GATEWAY

Dr. Thomas Walker

and the

Opening of Kentucky

David M. Burns

Photographs by Adam Jones
Introduction by Thomas D. Clark

Bell County (Kentucky) Historical Society   2000

This book is a publication of the
Bell County Historical Society
P.O. Box 1344
Middlesboro, Kentucky 40965 USA

Web Site:
http://www.geocities.com/Heartland/Hills/1810/

Telephone orders: (606) 242-0005
Toll-free number for orders: (877) 257-4844
Fax orders: (606) 242-0005
Orders by e-mail: *Bellhist_Society@hotmail.com*

Book edited and designed by Patrick C. Burns.

Library of Congress Catalog Number 99-085874
David M. Burns. Photographs by Adam Jones. Introduction by Thomas D. Clark.
Gateway: Dr. Thomas Walker and the Opening of Kentucky.
100 pp.   30 *cm* tall x 22.5 *cm* wide
Includes illustrations, maps, bibliography and index
ISBN 0-9677765-1-1
1. Dr. Thomas Walker. VA and KY History -- 18th century.
2. Cumberland Gap, Pine Mountain Gap, Cumberland Ford (KY).
3. The Wilderness Road, early settlement of Kentucky.
4. Land speculation -- The Loyal Company of Virginia.

Manufactured in the United States of America
First Edition

COVER: Walker with his wounded dog. *Journal*, April 7th: "We rode 8 miles over broken Land. It snowed most of the day. In the evening our dogs caught a large He Bear, which before we could come up to shoot him had wounded a dog of mine, so that he could not Travel, and we carried him on Horseback, till he recovered."

Proclamation

by

Paul E. Patton
Governor

of the

Commonwealth of Kentucky

Paul E. Patton
Governor
Commonwealth of Kentucky

To All To Whom These Presents Shall Come:

WHEREAS, Dr. Thomas Walker, physician and surveyor, together with five companions, was engaged by the Loyal Land Company to locate an 800,000-acre grant in "The Wilderness" beyond the forbidding and precipitous Appalachian Mountains; and

WHEREAS, Dr. Walker and his party, in April 1750, discovered Cumberland Gap, discovered and named the Cumberland River, discovered Pine Mountain Gap ("The Narrows"), and Cumberland Ford where horses and wagons could easily cross the river into Central Kentucky; and

WHEREAS, Dr. Walker built the first cabin in Kentucky near Barbourville; and

WHEREAS, Dr. Walker's discoveries of the two Gaps and The Ford opened a Triple Natural Gateway, making the Wilderness Road possible; and

WHEREAS, Dr. Walker's courage and resourcefulness showed America The Way West; his Journal and maps were critically-important to the migration of pioneer settlers into "The Great Meadow" of Kentucky; and

WHEREAS, An Historic Site commemorating Dr. Walker's discoveries will be dedicated near Pine Mountain State Resort Park on April 15, 2000: the Site will encourage us to study our past, stimulate the curiosity of tourists, excite the imagination of students to learn about Native Americans, explorers and settlers, and foster pride in our ancestors and heritage;

NOW, THEREFORE, I, PAUL E. PATTON, Governor of the Commonwealth of Kentucky, do hereby proclaim April 15, 2000 as

OPENING OF KENTUCKY DAY

In Kentucky and urge all Kentuckians to celebrate our history, honor Dr. Thomas Walker, and remember the Pioneers who bravely ventured into an unknown "Wilderness" to create better lives for us, their descendants.

DONE AT THE CAPITOL, in the City of Frankfort, this the 29th day of June, in the year of Our Lord One Thousand Nine Hundred Ninety-nine and in the 207TH year of the Commonwealth.

PAUL E. PATTON
GOVERNOR

John Y. Brown, III
Secretary of State

A Kentucky Historian Reflects

Through aeons of time the rising and falling of land surfaces in the area which is now Kentucky-Tennessee-Virginia opened an important passageway in the rocky spine of the eastern ridge of Pine Mountain range. In legend and rumor this gap became the gateway to the new "Western Eden." Through the centuries herbivorous animals and primitive man had tramped a trail through the pass. In the mid-eighteenth century the trail beckoned irresistibly to explorers.

By 1745 there was a brisk stirring of social, economic and political interests in the western lands. British and colonial Indian traders were able to compete stoutly with their French counterparts. The industrial revolution in England made it possible to supply trade goods in almost inexhaustible quantities and traders were penetrating ever-deeper into the western littoral. Too, the rising colonial American population exerted a continual pressure against the virginal frontier.

This fact was not lost on the speculators of the London Board of Trade, or those in the mid-colonies.

In 1744 there was negotiated one of the most significant treaties in American frontier history. Representatives from Pennsylvania, Virginia, and the six Indian tribes gathered at Lancaster, Pennsylvania and hammered out an agreement which opened a vast swath of frontier western land to future Euro-American claims and exploitation.

From the Carolinas to Pennsylvania, the settlement line was pushed westward. Indian traders, long hunters, and adventurers became increasingly aware that the trail through the Great Valley of Virginia led far beyond the Valley itself. This had been a matter of knowledge derived from various sources dating back to 1716 and Governor Spottswood and his "Knights of the Golden Horseshoe." Two prisoners of the Cherokee Indians, James Needham and Gabriel Arthur, were taken to the headwater region of the Tennessee River system. There they gathered information on the Indians, the land, and the trails.

Vast areas of land, apparently free for the taking, served as a magnet, drawing adventurers and speculators, stimulating the urge to explore the western backwoods. In the late 1740s, organized land companies were sending exploring parties westward, and a rivalry had developed between the Board of Trade and colonial entrepreneurs.

Thomas D. Clark
Historian-Laureate of Kentucky

The Loyal Land Company was created by Virginians centered in Albemarle County and the Charlottesville area. This Company's chief explorer was Dr. Thomas Walker, a man of several interests. He was said to have attended William and Mary College, studied medicine under the tutelage of a physician, and practiced medicine; he was a merchant, an exporter, and "a landed gentleman." When the Loyal Company was awarded a grant of 800,000 acres of western lands, Thomas Walker was the logical choice to lead the exploration. His surveying party of himself and five others, traveled west-ward on horseback, packhorses bearing their equipment and supplies. In April 1750, just as trees and shrubs were beginning to bud, the party traveled up the buffalo-Indian trail into the saddle of what they called Cave Gap.

On April 13, Walker noted in his Journal his sense of the magic and mystery of having arrived at a major dividing line between east and west.

He stood in the great Gap, a Gateway which in time would be trampled by literally thousands of land-hungry immigrants in search of the rich "new Eden."

Walker and his party recorded evidence that they were not the first Euro-American to pass that way. They discovered crosses and other markings on trees which were not of Indian origin. The group could not claim to having discovered the Gap. But Thomas Walker did stake an indelible claim in American frontier history by making a careful documentary record of his party's passage. His Journal, which has been published several times, is seminal in the history of the westward movement.

One can only speculate on what might have happened if Walker and his party had followed the Great Warrior's Trace, instead of turning west down the Cumberland River. Would they have reached the heartland of Kentucky? The explorers followed the rugged course of the river to a point in present-day Knox County, where they built a crude cabin. This was their point of desperation, however: they turned eastward into the craggy Rockcastle River country where Thomas Walker described the discovery of a huge "rock overhang," or castle, which can still be viewed much as he would have seen it in the spring of 1750. They crossed the Kentucky River headlands, and struggled back over the trackless mountains of present-day West Virginia.

As a land-hunting expedition, the Walker venture must be considered a failure. But the venture was a success in that the party passed through two great gaps and recorded their observations. They followed the well-padded trail through "Cave Gap" and to the river. Along the way, Walker made journalistic descriptions of still-identifiable landmarks. He gave a name and a symbol to the American westward movement — the name "Cumberland." It is an anomaly of American history that the victor of the bloody Battle of Culloden should be given such prominence. Walker named the Gap, the Mountain, and the River for the Duke. And Kentuckians later followed Walker's lead and gave the name to a county, a town, a college, a branch of the Presbyterian Church, numerous commercial enterprises, and a National Forest.

No historian can assert with documentary assurance that any of the many, but nameless, long hunters who roamed the western woods ever knew about the Walker expedition or read his Journal. It is doubtful that so prominent a western adventurer as Daniel Boone knew about Thomas Walker's Journal, though he surely knew of Walker, the surveyor. What was most significant was that Walker and his companions traversed the Gap and noted the fact in writing. Boone popularized the name Cumberland Gap in history, and more than 300,000 travelers tramped a Road of great importance in the American frontier legacy.

> **Walker stood in the great Gap, a Gateway which in time would be trampled by literally thousands of land-hungry immigrants in search of the rich "new Eden."**

Walker's name was firmly imprinted on the western slopes of the Appalachians, though he established no claim to the vast acreage of western lands, founded no settlement, nor lived in the country. In 1779, he served as one of two Virginia representatives who, with two North Carolina delegates including Richard Henderson, negotiated an agreement on the extension of the North Carolina-Virginia boundary westward to Pine Mountain. West of the mountain, Walker surveyed the line to the Tennessee river. This boundary remained in contention until it was resurveyed and marked by Cox-Peebles in 1860.

An oddity in Kentucky history is that no county has been named for Thomas Walker, no mountain or river, no town, no forest preserve. Yet, he must be credited as one of the "openers" of an important geological passageway in the history of the expanding American civilization.

— **Thomas D. Clark**

Geology of the Two Gaps

The Rocks

The rocks that later became the Appalachian mountains were created in a variety of environments. Many of the underlying rock layers are limestone and shale formed 330 to 320 million years ago. The limestone was formed in shallow seas as sand from broken sea shells and coral. Over time, as groundwater percolated through the sediment, the limey sands were cemented into stone by calcite. The shales originated as mud on the bottom of shallow seas; when the mud was compressed by the overlying rock, water was squeezed out, forming shale.

> **Without Rocky Face fault, water could not have carved the gaps and the two mountains would have remained impenetrable cliffs.**

The Mountains

Pine Mountain and Cumberland Mountain form part of the Appalachian range, extending from northern Alabama to Nova Scotia. The two mountains are about a hundred and twenty miles long, ten to fifteen miles apart, parallel to each other and to the Kentucky-Virginia border. The Appalachian chain was formed 245 million years ago when the African plate collided with the North American plate. This inexorable force slowly buckled Eastern North America, uplifting a long chain of towering peaks. Today, after millions of years of erosion, the Appalachians are dramatically diminished, a fraction of their original height.

When the surface was flat, what is today called Yellow Creek flowed south into the Powell River. As the Cumberland Mountain was pushed up, the Creek cut a notch (Cumberland Gap). But the mountain rose more rapidly than the Creek could erode and the flowing water was eventually diverted northward into the Cumberland.

Rocks on the crest of Pine Mountain, such as Chained Rock, a tourist attraction at Pineville, were deposited as river sand about 320 million years ago. Both Pine Mountain and Cumberland Mountain resisted erosion because they were overlain by these hard sandstones.

The Gaps

In addition to bending and uplifting rock, the African-North American collision also created faults — that is, breaks in the crust of the earth. Rocky Face, which can be seen from U.S. 25-E halfway between Middlesboro and Pineville, is a prominent sandstone ridge and a visible sign of this otherwise invisible rip in the fabric of the earth.

Rocky Face fault, named after the ridge, is a lateral (side-ways) break, not an uplift. Rocky Face, Pine Mountain Gap and Cumberland Gap are aligned in a north-south direction, whereas the two mountains are aligned, like virtually all Appalachian ridges, in a southwest-northeast direction. Rocky Face fault exposed softer rock such as shale, and created access for water. The softer rocks were easily carved creating the historically important Gaps — Cumberland Gap and Pine Mountain Gap ("the Narrows").

Coal

About 310 million years ago, vast swamp forests were forming Kentucky's coal deposits. Dr. Walker notes in his *Journal* that he found coal in Bell and Knox counties and elsewhere, and brought back samples — perhaps to prove to The Loyal Company that there was, indeed, something of economic worth on the western side of the Mountains. There are records of coal being mined in Kentucky since the 1790s.

Middlesboro Basin

The Middlesboro Basin is probably the result of a meteor impact about 300 million years ago. So much debris has eroded into the basin, however, it is impossible to identify the meteor itself.

■

TOP: raised-relief map of Cumberland Gap and Pine Gap. Rocky Face Fault underlies the low ridge aligned with both gaps in a north-south direction. **LOWER PHOTO** shows the topography of eastern Kentucky, with Pine Mountain prominent. Cumberland Mountain is aligned with it and straddles the Kentucky-Virginia border. **The Cumberland River, a dark line along the south side of Pine Mountain, cuts through Pine Mountain at "The Narrows" gorge. This Gap is the critical second Gateway of The Wilderness Road.**

Trails of Animals, Extinct & Extant

Long hunters, and Dr. Thomas Walker and his companions, followed animal and Indian trails through the two Gaps. The animal trails were first made by species now extinct: woolly mammoths, mastodons, ground sloths, immense stag moose, and giant "buffalo" (American bison). These Ice Age animals retreated southward as the glaciers crept down from Canada, stopping just north of present day Cincinnati.

In the Ice Age climate, large animals tended to fare better as they could store vast quantities of fat to maintain warmth, while exposing less surface area to the cold.

> **When John James Audubon was sketching birds in Kentucky in 1815, the sky was often black with millions of passenger pigeons. The last one died in The Cincinnati Zoo in 1914.**

Humans entered Alaska some 40,000-15,000 years ago (exact dates are intensely debated). Paleo-Indian "mammoth hunters" roamed over North America, including Kentucky, about 13,000 years ago. They were skilled in attacking giant Ice-Age animals with handheld spears. Within a few centuries, climate change and relentless hunting had exterminated mastodons and mammoths, the largest American mammals.

Giant Ice Age bison, considerably larger than their modern counterparts, met a similar fate. *Bison latifrons*, with twelve-foot horns, died out some 300,000 years ago as climate and habitat changed, and *Bison antiquus* (twenty per cent heavier than the modern species) was hunted to extinction by Indians about 10,000 years ago (climate may also have been a factor).

There may have been sixty million bison in North America 170 years ago. Eastern woodlands bison were extinct in Kentucky about 1810, and larger Western plains bison barely survived. Nineteenth-century Indians themselves came perilously close to annihilation.

Walker's *Journal* boasts of the prodigious number of animals his group killed. The resources of "The Wilderness" may have seemed so abundant, they perhaps could not imagine humans would ever have much impact.

Bison latifrons, Bison antiquus

Long hunters shot as much as they could. Deer and elk hides, and beaver, bison and bear pelts fetched a good price. Game was also vital for settlers. Their survival, at least in their first years, depended on what they could kill until they could "make a crop." And game remained an important source of food and clothing.

Today and Tomorrow

The future of modern fauna in the Cumberland Mountains is unclear. Preservation of habitat is vital if we care enough to save remnant species from our relentless will to waste. But in many parts of Kentucky today deer are so plentiful they are a nuisance. Fox, groundhog, raccoon, possum, squirrel, chipmunk, and skunk are ubiquitous. Wild turkey and beaver are increasingly seen. Black bear are migrating in from West Virginia and Tennessee.

Otter have been reintroduced and seem to be doing well. Elk imported from refuge areas in the West have been reintroduced into Eastern Kentucky; they are reproducing and may become established. European boar were introduced in 1912, but can be mistaken for domestic swine that have gone wild. The wolf, fisher-marten and mountain lion are gone. ■

Woolly mammoth and baby

Dawn, Powell Valley, from The Pinnacle overlook atop Cumberland Gap.

Ice Age mammals traversed the Gaps, migrating for food. Many remains are found at Big Bone Lick, Kentucky. Photo shows the molar of a woolly mammoth (adults weighed ten tons or more, and some were fourteen feet high at the shoulder), the femur of a giant sloth (twelve feet long, six feet high), and the jawbone of *Bison Antiquus*.

Land of Cane and Clover

When Walker and other explorers entered what is now eastern Kentucky, the landscape was primarily a climax hardwood forest dominated by chestnut, oak, hickory, beech, and maple. It was a luxuriant "closed" forest with the most biological diversity of any biome in North America. Only tiny remnants of the original forest remain, such as Blanton Forest in Harlan County, and Lilley Cornett Woods in Letcher County.

> **The first thing a settler did was chop down as many trees as he could and burn the stumps.**

The virgin forest produced profuse acorns and chestnuts which sustained huge populations of black bear and other animals. Deer were more often found on the grassy "bald knobs," created when Indians burned the hilltops.

To early settlers, forests were a hindrance to travel, obstacles to homebuilding and farming, and a hiding place for hostile Indians. The first thing a settler did was chop down as many trees as he could and burn the stumps. "Fire on the mountain" was not just a song. Cedar and chestnut provided logs for a cabin, shakes for roofing and rails for fences. Trees that remained were used to heat the cabin, make ashes for lye soap, or charcoal for iron production. A settler's clearing was usually devoid of trees, for protection and to "make a crop." Chestnuts were killed, 1904-34, by a fungus blight. Today, oak and hickory dominate Kentucky forests.

Long hunters used chestnut and oak bark, and acorns to obtain *tannic acid* for tanning elk and deer hides, which they hauled out on packhorses for sale in the East. The tanning process was carried out in creek beds.

Carcasses were left to rot, hence names like "Greasy Creek" and "Stinking Creek."

Commercial lumbering took a dramatic toll, particularly from 1880 to 1910, when production peaked. Kentucky has supplied sawn timber to the nation and the world for a century and a half. Rowan County in Eastern Kentucky is still the leading producer of hardwood in the United States.

Many trees — white and red oak, basswood, hemlock — were huge. Magnificent tulip poplar, up to ten feet in diameter, soared 200 feet high, the tallest hardwood species in America. Great rafts of logs were floated to sawmills down the Kentucky, Big Sandy and Tug Fork rivers. Trees that fetched the highest price were black walnut and other hardwoods for furniture. Later, hickory and oak were sought out for railroad ties, and as strong roof props for coal mines. Some hardwood was used for aircraft carrier decks.

In his *Journal*, Walker writes of river and creek banks choked with near-impassable "canebrakes." This woody reed, *Arundinaria*, is Kentucky's only bamboo; it can still be found, though no longer abundant or dense. Bison fattened on cane shoots, as did pioneer cattle. Filson and other early map-makers mark vast areas of "cane," thought to be an indication of fertile land, suitable for farming.

Walker also writes of "beargrass," and gives that name to the river we now call the Powell. It is not clear what plant he had in mind. "Clover Creek" may refer to Buffalo Clover, a plant recently rediscovered in Kentucky, and very rare. Walker also writes of hacking through "laurel" thickets; what we now call rhododendron. Conversely, Walker's "ivy" is now called mountain laurel. ■

CANE, a woody reed, *Arundinaria*, Kentucky's only bamboo. Explorers describe river and creek banks choked with impassable "canebrakes" so impenetrable they had to hack their way through with "tomahawks." Bison and cattle fattened on the shoots. Early maps of Kentucky show vast areas of "cane," thought to indicate fertile land.

Sell the Air? the Sky? the Water?

"Indians" were the first Americans. They were hunters, following Ice Age mammals from Siberia to Alaska, then fanning out over two continents. Over many centuries they became separate groups, diverse in language and culture. They had no weapons or tools except those of wood, bone or stone; no wheeled vehicles; no domestic animals except dogs; no cloth; no energy source except their muscles, nor did they use sails; they had no written language.

> **Encounters between Europeans and Indians were a dialogue of the deaf, two cultures with entirely different and incompatible world-views.**

But they were keen observers of nature and used every thing the environment offered. Europeans recognized that Indians knew their land and how to use it far better than newcomers.

Encounters between Europeans and Indians were a dialogue of the deaf, two cultures with entirely different and incompatible world-views. The final outcome was never in doubt: Indians lost virtually everything. In return, they transformed the world: they gave us squash, beans, chocolate, and "the sot-weed," tobacco. Potatoes virtually eliminated famines in Europe, and population there expanded quickly. Maize (corn) is today one of the world's main food crops.

The gold and silver of the Aztecs and Incas transformed the mercantile system of Europe into true monetary capitalism, and for the first time there was a commodity other than land as the basis of wealth, power, and prestige.

It is not useful to romanticize Indians as environmental purists or as an ideal "primitive man." Indians did, however, believe they could exist only in cooperation with other elements of the environment. They saw themselves as related to all living things, and believed that every thing in Nature possessed a spirit. They knew they depended on animals for food, and went so far as to ask "forgiveness" of animals they killed, to show "respect" and elicit the animals' cooperation. Indians killed mainly to eat and wasted little. Customs were set by the tribe. Authority flowed from attributes like wisdom and bravery. Indian groups shared everything. Personal ownership was confined to a warrior's weapons and the squaw's wigwam. Who could "possess" Land?

When they were outnumbered, Europeans were forced to consider Indian views and deal with them by treaties. But Indians were decimated by European diseases such as smallpox. After Indians were outnumbered and outgunned, they were placed on reservations. The nation turned its attention to other matters.

Walker was considered by his Virginia contemporaries as having excellent relations with Indians, who frequently stopped to visit at his home and whom he treated with respect. He represented Virginia at negotiations which led to the Treaty of Fort Stanwix in 1768, and negotiated a new boundary line with the Cherokee, defined in the Treaty of Lochaber in 1770. The legislature appointed him to negotiate peace with the Shawnee after their defeat at the Battle of Point Pleasant in 1774, and he traveled to the site, where the Kanawha enters the Ohio River. He presided as commissioner at Fort Pitt for the treaty in 1775, and in 1777 returned with a Native American boy he planned to educate.

Old Tom, one of his slaves, said Walker lived with Indians for seven years, perhaps 1748-1754 when he spent much time near Wolf Hills [now Abingdon, VA]. Or perhaps when he was a participant in treaty negotiations.

[McLeod I, pp175-176] ■

Indian stone whistle, found in a Burial Mound at Pineville, KY.

Indian figurine in The Rock House, Pine Mountain State Resort Park. The statue was found in 1869 under a big cliff in Pine Mountain Gap. The figurine is now in the Museum of the American Indian, Washington, D.C. The wood is yellow pine; facial details are obliterated, but one ear is pierced as though for jewelry. *Replica carved by Lee Thomas Hopkins, loaned courtesy Mike Crockett. Replica on exhibit in Bell County Historical Society Museum.*

Indian Paths To Wilderness

Dr. Thomas Walker was not the first European into eastern Kentucky, though he was the first to write about it, and map it. On April 10, 1673, Abraham Wood, active in opening Virginia's western frontier to trade, sent out from Fort Henry *[present-day Petersburg]* a group led by James Needham, a South Carolina planter, explorer and Indian trader. Gabriel Arthur was Needham's assistant. We know few details about Arthur, perhaps because he could not read or write. But he is one of the first Europeans to travel The Warrior's Path and cross The Cumberland Gap.

Arthur was captured by Shawnee and taken North. When released in the spring of 1674, he was given an elk skin pouch of parched corn and conducted to a path south across the Bluegrass. The path led to The Great Gap, then southeast to Cherokee territory in the Carolina mountains.

> **With no money to pay veterans, the Continental Congress alloted them western land.**

There was little danger of getting lost: the trail was well-defined, called by Indians the *Athawominee*, "Path of the Armed Ones" ["Warrior's Path"]. It had been used for centuries by many tribes — on long hunts, for trade, and on raids of revenge or conquest. The Path was a major link in the Indian trail system, well-established long before Columbus discovered America.

The trail led Arthur into the Cumberland Mountains, called by the Wyandot and Shawnee *"Wasioto"* ["mountains where deer are plentiful"] and to Cumberland Gap. Arthur arrived back at Fort Henry on June 18, 1674, after more than a year's absence. But Wood did not realize the significance of Arthur's trip, or follow up.

Others include John Salling, a weaver from Williamsburg, who was captured in 1730 by Cherokee near Great Lick *[Roanoke]*. He was held by the tribe three years, and taken by them to the salt licks of Kentucky to hunt buffalo. He was captured again, this time by Indians from Illinois, and held two years. He eventually made his way back to Williamsburg via Canada and New York.

The Treaty of Paris ended the French and Indian War, and the Proclamation of 1763 was part of the Treaty. The British were given "possession" of land between the Appalachians and the Mississippi, but to appease the Indians agreed to limit settlements. Colonists, however, were not prepared to obey a piece of paper — not while fertile land was available and unused.

Settlement beyond the mountains began immediately. By the 1768 Treaty of Fort Stanwix *[present-day Rome, New York]*, in which Walker represented Virginia, the Six Nations (five Iroquois tribes, plus the Tuscarora) abandoned claim to all land (which they did not in fact control) to the Tennessee River and agreed to withdraw from land south of the Ohio River.

When the Revolutionary War ended, the Continental Congress was grateful to the sharp-shooters who won victory at the Battle of Kings Mountain. But the young nation had no money to pay them. So Congress allotted western lands to the unpaid veterans. It was a tremendous lure: free land, plentiful game, and few social and legal restraints. The war veteran strapped his rifle and few other possessions onto a mule or horse and, with wife and children plodding behind, climbed the hills and waded creeks until he found an area which seemed to suit.

Others also hungered for land. Indentured servants sweating on Tidewater tobacco plantations dreamed of vast farmland, free for the taking. They ran away to the interior, to the Piedmont, to the foothills of the Blue Ridge. They were joined by others who came when their contracts expired. And so they all set out.

These are the people, often living at first under cliffs or in rude cabins, who are the ancestors of the Southern mountaineers. They moved often, to areas with unplowed creek bottoms, or more plentiful game. In time, and with immigration, the steady stream turned into a flood. ■

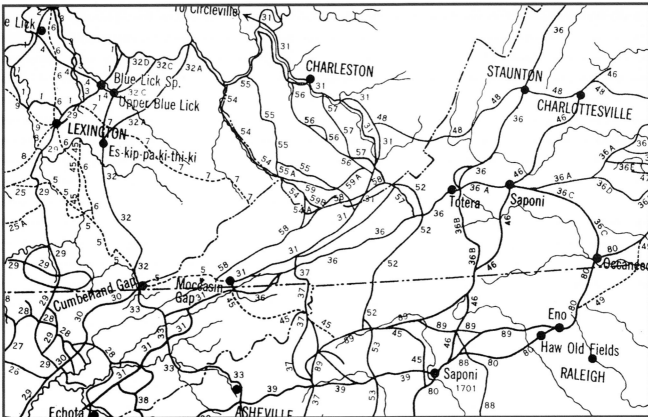

TOP: Crest of Cumberland Mountain from The Pinnacle.
BOTTOM: Indian trail system of the Southeastern United States in the Early Colonial Period.
Part of The Warrior's Path connected the powerful Iroquois Confederacy of Five Nations in the
North and the Cherokee and Catawba empires in the South. Walker followed several of these trails
and passes, including Moccasin Gap. But he did not turn north toward the Bluegrass, nor the Indian
trade town of *Eskippakithiki [near present-day Winchester, KY].*

Guns, Germs, and Survival

The struggle between Europeans and Indians for control of North America began at contact and continued for more than three hundred years. The two cultures stood in relation to each other much as chestnut forests stood in relation to the chestnut blight.

Conquest by European gunpowder and steel was not new or unique: Australian Aborigines and Africans were also conquered, displaced, or decimated.

> **By 1750, the colonial population was doubling every 25 years, while the Indian population had crashed to one-sixth its original size.**

The most persuasive explanation for unequal development — specifically, European technology vs. "primitive natives" — is found in *Guns, Germs and Steel: The Fates of Human Societies*. Jared Diamond argues that geography is destiny or, more fully: "the striking differences between the long-term histories of people of the different continents have been due not to innate differences in the peoples themselves, but to differences in their environments." *[p405]*

By 1750 a chain of English colonies stretched along the Atlantic coast. They contained over a million people of European or African origin, with the population doubling every twenty-five years. The push of people made it crucial to open the western frontier — which Dr. Thomas Walker and The Loyal Company were quite happy to do. Exploration and speculation was of benefit to all, since a continual supply of good farming land guaranteed general growth and prosperity. Land was the goal of every settler.

The Indian population, however, was in rapid decline. Of the estimated 120,000 in the thirteen colonies when they were first settled, perhaps 20,000 remained *[McEvedy p52]*. Thousands had been killed by frontier wars or by European diseases, especially smallpox and tuberculosis.

Indians had to be mobile in order to "gather" the resources of their environment, and mobility required that they own and carry little. Also, as hunters, they required a low population density. An Indian family needed as many square miles as a colonial family did acres.

John Quincy Adams said what many felt: "What is the right of a huntsman to the forest of a thousand miles over which he has accidentally ranged in search of prey? Shall the fields and vallies, which a beneficent God has formed to teem with the life of innumerable multitudes, be condemned to everlasting barrenness?"

Europeans concluded that Indians were unworthy of the rich land they happened to occupy and that, in seizing the land, they were obeying the Biblical injunction to "fill the earth and subdue it." To Europeans, Indians lived like beggars in the midst of great natural abundance. They took the Indian paucity of goods as proof of their laziness and backwardness — tangible confirmation of their savage, alien character.

As game was shot out or trapped out, one of the few things Indians had left to sell was their skill in fighting — and Europeans were quick to employ that skill. Indians were recruited as allies by both France and Britain. Most worked for the French until 1773. But they then switched sides and began to work with the British. In both cases, the motivation was money and the hope of ejecting settlers.

The Indian style of warfare — lightning ambushes, swift raids, cold cruelty — seemed the work of devils. Indian raids terrorized the settlers, who demonized the Indians by endlessly repeating stories replete with detailed descriptions of torture and brutality. Women and children were as likely to fall victim to Indian raids as were fighting men. Life was dangerous even in the forts. If defeated, the Kentuckians faced death, captivity and torture, or flight back east. Settlers had to fight, win, and survive, and they did. Ultimately, it was Cherokees, not settlers, who were forced to walk "The Trail of Tears." ∎

Rock House, Pine Mountain State Resort Park. Indian Woodlands groups, several thousand years ago, often used rockshelters. They cultivated hillside garden plots, though game may have been their main diet. Walker wrote in his *Journal*, April 18, 1750: "Indians have lived about this Ford some years ago." He may have been alluding to the burial mound four hundred yards from the Ford of the Cumberland River *[Pineville, Kentucky]*. The mound was probably made by the Woodlands people. The top of the mound was removed in 1900 to make a house foundation. The remainder of the mound was removed in 1987 to create space for a Kentucky Fried Chicken restaurant.

Six Men, Eight Horses, Five Dogs

From *The Journal* of Dr. Thomas Walker:

"Having, on the 12th day of December last, been employed for a certain consideration to go to the Westward in order to discover a proper Place for a Settlement, I left my house on the Sixth day of March at 10 o'clock, 1749-50 *[the two years relate to Julian and Gregorian calendars, one used in America, the other in England]*, in company with Ambrose Powell, William Tomlinson, Colby Chew, Henry Lawless, and John Hughs. Each man had a Horse and we had two to carry the baggage. I lodged this night at Col. Joshua Fry's, in Albemarle which county includes the head Branches of James River on the East side of the Blue Ridge."

> *"This lick has been one of the best places for Game ... and would have been of much greater advantage to the inhabitants if hunters had not killed the Buffaloes for diversion, and Elks and Deer for their skins."*

"**March 7th** ...The day proving wet, we only went to Thomas Joplin's at Rockfish. This is a pretty River, which might at small expense be made fit to transport tobacco; but it has lately been stopped by a small Mill Dam near the mouth to the prejudice of the upper inhabitants who would at their own expense clear and make it navigable, were they permitted."

"**March 8th.** We left Joplin's early. It began to rain about noon. I went to the Reverend Mr. Robert Rose's on Tye River, about the size of Rockfish, as yet open, but how long the Avarice of Millers will permit it to be so, I know not. The Inhabitants enjoy plenty of fine fish, as Shad in Season, Carp, Rocks, Fat-Backs, Perch, Mullets, etc."

"**13th.** We went early to William Calloway's and supplied ourselves with Rum, Thread, and other necessaries and from thence took the main waggon road leading to the Wood's or the New River. It is not well clear'd or beaten yet, but will be a very good one with proper management. This night we lodged in Adam Beard's ... Beard is an ignorant, imprudent, brutish fellow, and would have taken us up *[beaten and robbed us]*, had it not been for a reason easily to be suggested."

"**14th.** We went to Nicholas Welches, where we bought corn for our horses, and had some Victuals dress'd for dinner, afterwards we crossed the Blue Ridge. The Ascent and Descent is so easie a stranger would not know when he crossed the Ridge. It began to rain about noon and continued until night. We lodged at William Armstrong's. Corn is very scarce in these parts."

"**15th.** We went to the great Lick *[Roanoke]* on a branch of the Staunton & bought corn of Michael Campbell for our Horses. This afternoon we got to the Staunton where the Houses of the Inhabitants had been carryed off with their grain and Fences by the Fresh *[flood]* last summer, and lodged at James Robinson's, the only place I could hear of where they had corn to spare, notwithstanding the land is such that an industrious man might make 100 barrels a share in a Seasonable year."

"**16th March.** We kept up the Staunton to William Englishes. He lives on a small Branch, and was not much hurt by the Fresh. He has a mill, which is the furthest back except one lately built by the Sect of People, who call themselves of the Brotherhood of Euphrates ... commonly called Duncards'."

"**20th** ... Purchased half a bushell of meal and as much small homony ..."

"**March 21st**. We ... camped near James McCalls'. I went to his House and Lodged and bought what Bacon I wanted."

"**23rd**. We kept down Holston River ... and went to look for Samuel Stalnaker."

"**24th**: We helped him raise his house." *[Stalnaker's was shown on the Fry-Jefferson map (1751) as the limit of western settlement.]* ∎

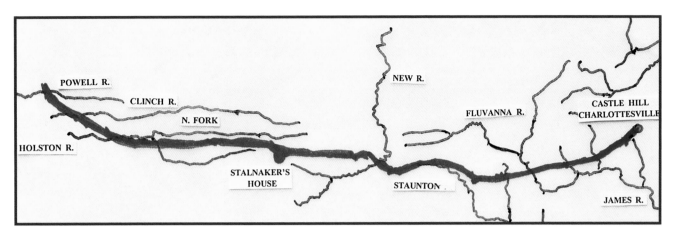

Route of Dr. Walker and his five companions from Charlottesville to the Powell River. "Stalnaker's House" was mentioned on several early maps and was considered the limit of western settlement of the Colony of Virginia.

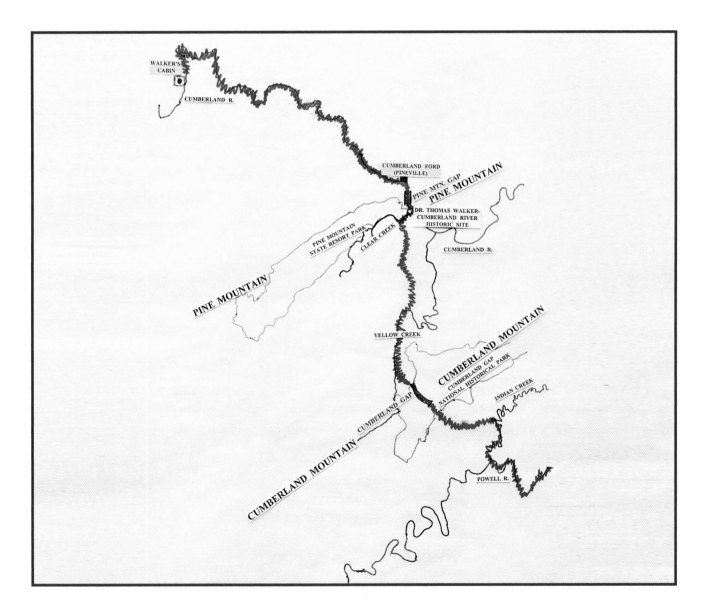

Walker's route from the Powell Valley: Cumberland Gap, along Yellow Creek, to Clear Creek, through Pine Mountain Gap, and to Cumberland Ford *[present-day Pineville, Kentucky]*. They then continued along the river, and built a cabin.

Beargrass, Cave Gap, Cumberland

"**March 31st**. We kept down Reedy Creek to Holston where we measured an elm 25 feet around 3 feet from the ground ... In the Fork are five Indian Houses built with loggs and covered with Bark, and there were abundance of Bones, some whole pots and pans, some broken, and many pieces of mats and cloth. On the West side of the North River, is four Indian Houses such as before mentioned."

> *"We camped on the bank where we found very good Coal. We rode 13 miles this day."*

"**April 5th**. There is much Holly in the Low Grounds & some Laurel and Ivy."

"**April 7th** ... 8 miles over broken Land. It snowed most of the day. In the evening our dogs caught a large He Bear, which before we could come up to shoot him had wounded a dog of mine, so that he could not Travel, and we carried him on Horseback, till he recovered."

"**April 12th** ...We rode four miles to Beargrass *[Powell]* River. Small Cedar Trees are very plenty. . .and some Barberry trees on the East side of the river. On the banks is some Bear-Grass. We kept up the river two miles, I found some small pieces of coal and a great plenty of very good yellow flint. The water is the most transparent I ever saw ... about 70 yards wide."

"**April 13th**. We went four miles to a large Creek, which we called Cedar Creek, being a branch of Bear-Grass, and from thence six miles to Cave *[Cumberland]* Gap the land being levil. On the north side of the gap is a large Spring, which falls very fast, and just above the Spring is a small entrance to a large Cave, which the Spring runs through, and there is a constant Stream of cool air issuing out. The Spring is sufficient to turn a Mill. Just at the foot of the Hill is a Laurel Thicket, and the Spring Water runs through it. On the South side is a plain Indian Road. On top of the Ridge are Laurel Trees marked with crosses, others blazed and several figures on them ... A Beech stands on the left hand, on which I cut my name. The North Side of the Gap is very Steep and Rocky, but on the South side it is not so. We called it Steep Ridge. At the foot of the hill on the North West side we came to a Branch, that made a great deal of flat Land. We kept down it 2 miles, several other branches coming in to make it a large Creek, and we called it Flat *[Yellow]* Creek. We camped on the bank where we found very good Coal. We rode 13 miles this day."

"**April 14**. We kep down the Creek 5 miles Chiefly along the Indian Road."

"**15th**. East Sunday. Being in bad ground for our Horses we moved 7 miles along the Indian Road, to Clover *[Clear]* Creek. Clover and hop vines are plenty here."

"**April 16th**. Rain. I made a pair of Indian

Shoes, those I brought being bad."

"**17th.** Still Rain. I went down the Creek a hunting and found that it went into a River about a mile below our Camp. This, which is Flat Creek and some others join'd, I called Cumberland River."

"**18th**. Still cloudy. We kept down the Creek to the River along the Indian Road to where it crosses. Indians have lived about this Ford some years ago. We kept down the south Side. After riding 5 miles from our Camp we left the River, it being very crooked ... 60 or 70 yards wide."

"**23rd** We all crossed the River ... leaving the other to provide and salt some Bear, build an house and plant some Peach Stones and Corn. We got through the coal today." ■

Profile of Cumberland Mountain from Powell Valley. Walker followed the valleys of the Shenandoah, Holston, Clinch and "Beargrass" [Powell] rivers. Walker followed Indian Creek up a well-trod Buffalo-Indian Road to "Cave Gap." He reached Cumberland Gap 19 years before Daniel Boone. Long hunters proceeded them both.

Shawnee River, Ouasioto Gap

"The Great Wilderness" was the term used by hunters for the mountain country, today called The Cumberland Plateau. High ridges, steep cliffs and swift rivers made for hard going even for expert rough-country frontiersmen. To this was added anxiety about the possibility of capture and torture by Shawnee Indians, resolutely guarding an area they regarded as "their" hunting grounds.

Long hunters coming from Virginia called the first break in the mountain "Cave Gap." Twelve miles farther on was a river, known as "The Shawnee," and shown as such on early French maps, including Jacque Bellin's "Carte de la Louisiane" (1744). As late as 1765, Captain Gordon's drawings of the Ohio River still refer to the river as "Shawnee." The surrounding mountains were "Wasioto" *[Shawnee or Wyandot, "land where deer are plentiful"]*. Wasioto was also the name of the Gap at Pine Mountain.

There is little doubt that Walker knew the names used by hunters and Indians for these geographical features. This was not his first trip to the area: in 1748, he was part of Colonel James Patton's exploration of southwest Virginia for the Wood River Land Company. Walker's *Journal* makes clear he knew where to find Stalnaker's settlement. And his *Journal* refers immediately to "Cave Gap."

But why would he re-name the river? Walker was dedicated to the western expansion of Virginia. Calling the river "Shawnee" would support Indian claims and deter fearful settlers. Giving the river a good English name honoring British royalty might benefit The Company, and his own speculative interest.

"Walker's settlement, 1750" [one tiny cabin] was noted on almost all subsequent maps, including the Fry-Jefferson map (1751), printed in London 1754, and a French map by Robert de Vaugondy in 1755, as "Walker's establiss Anglois."

Walker furnished details of terrain, streams and trails for Lewis Evans' 1755 "Map of the Middle British Colonies," revised 1776 by Thomas Pownall. The two maps show "Ouasioto Mountains" in present-day Kentucky and West Virginia: "A Vein of Mountains about 30 or 40 Miles right across through which there is not yet any occupied Path in these Parts." Stalnaker's is shown between the Middle and South Forks of the Holston, called "the farthest Settlement in Virginia in 1755." *[Clark, Historic Maps of KY, pp 2-3.]*

From Thomas Pownall's 1776 edition of the Lewis and Jefferson map (see page 14).

Judge William Ayers of Pineville wrote in 1924: "There is but one water-gap in the Pine Range and that is the great gorge at Pineville ..." The pioneer saw "Pine Mountain forming a barrier ... But as he advanced along the foot of the Mountain, he came to the spot at the mouth of Clear Creek where the Cumberland River, flowing southwestward along the foot of Pine Range, turns right to a northward course. At the outer angle of this bend Clear Creek enters, and here is the spot upon which Thomas Walker stood in 1750 when he caught his first sight of the river which in his journal entry he names `Cumberland River.'" *[Ayers, 1924]*

Walker writes that "Indians have lived about this Ford." One bit of evidence was the burial mound about four hundred yards from the Ford. Ayers says the Indians were "a southern branch of the Mound Builders whose most famous works are near Chillicothe, Ohio. The mound top was removed in 1900 to build a house for Dr. Fuson." ■

Clear Creek, at the spot where Walker discovered and named the Cumberland river in April 1750. The Dr. Thomas Walker-Cumberland River Historic Site overlooks the confluence and offers a spectacular view of "The Narrows" [Ouasioto Gap].

Walker's Journal: *"Laurel rather growing worse. Mountains very bad, tops of the ridges so covered with Ivy and the sides so steep and stony, obliged to cut our way through with our Tomohawks. Creek so full of Laurel obliged to go up a Branch. Laurel thickest I have seen."*

Sunrise from the crest of Pine Mountain. Pine Mountain State Resort Park offers many stunning views of the ridges and valleys of the Cumberland Plateau.

Peach Stones and Seed Corn

**From *The Journal* of
Dr. Thomas Walker:**

"**April 22nd.** The Sabbath. One of the horses was found unable to walk this morning. I then Propos'd that with 2 of the Company I would proceed, and the other three should continue here till our return, which was agreed to, and Lots were drawn to determine who should go, they all being desirous of it. Ambrose Powell, and Colby Chew were the fortunate Persons ..."

> **The building of a "house" and planting of corn and peaches, was to establish a claim of settlement [or "corn rights"] on behalf of The Loyal Company.**

"**23rd**. Having carried our Baggage over in the Bark Canoe, and Swam our horses, we all crossed the River. Then Ambrose Powell, Colby Chew, and I departed, leaving the others to provide and salt some Bear, build an house, and plant some Peach Stones and Corn. We travelled about 12 miles ... We got through the Coal today."

Dr. Walker left his fellow explorers at a "bottom" of fertile land a few hundred yards from the newly-named "Cumberland" River near present-day Barbourville, Kentucky. Walker knew he was not the first English colonial to enter Kentucky. But he was the first to keep a *Journal* and make notes for a map. The building of a "house" and planting of corn and peaches, was to establish a claim of settlement [or "corn rights"] on behalf of The Loyal Company.

Walker encountered more rough country after leaving his three companions. On April 25, he wrote: "the land continuing much the same, The Laurel rather growing worse and food scarcer. I got up a tree on a ridge and saw the growth of the land much the same as far as my sight could reach. I then concluded to return to the rest of my company." Walker and his party were in rugged terrain made more difficult of passage by tangled laurel thickets and canebrakes. Harriette Simpson Arnow, in *Seedtime on the Cumberland*, writes: the cane grew "thirty feet tall and three inches thick." It was hard to get through the "miserable stuff, crowding in a close wall twenty feet high and more, shutting out light and air, forever bending enough to whip a rider in the face." *[pp 20, 221]*

On April 28, Walker returned to the site where he had left the three others: His *Journal* notes: "The people I left had built a house 8 x 12, cleared and broke up some ground and planted corn and peach stones. They had also killed several bears and cured the meat."

This was the first house built by Europeans in Kentucky and the farthest west of colonial civilization of that day.

The cabin, with additions, was occupied until 1835, but had long vanished when the site was located by a worker on the Louisville & Nashville Railroad. A marker was placed in 1922, and a replica of pioneer log huts of the period was built in 1932. The replica stands on a 12-acre Historic Site, a Kentucky State Park. The cabin is of round logs with wide chinked joints and a small end chimney, oddly framed at the base with notched logs. The door is of rough slabs pegged together and hinged in early pioneer fashion without iron. Other items are a one-post triple-decked bed, three-legged stools, and, on the exterior, a skinning pole and salting trough to dress and cure game.

"This day Colby Chew and his horse fell down the bank. I bled and gave him volatile drops and soon he recovered." They started back April 30, first north, then through present-day West Virginia, back toward the Piedmont.

Walker turned back just short of the rolling Bluegrass. His report to the Loyal Company was unfavorable, and the Company did not "enter" the lands it was granted west of the mountains. But The Company remained active in western land speculation for many more decades. ∎

Eastern Woodlands Bison were killed by Indians and settlers for pelts and for food. They were extinct in Kentucky by about 1810.

REPLICA OF

FIRST HOUSE

IN KENTUCKY

Walker's eight-foot by twelve-foot cabin (replica above in Dr. Thomas Walker State Park, near Barbourville, Kentucky), was shown on maps after 1751. The cabin was a "claim marker" for The Loyal Company's grant of 800,000 acres of western frontier land.

Journal Exerpts, From The Cabin

Walker, Colby Chew and Ambrose Powell leave. Walker writes: "**April 24, 1750**: We got clear of the Mountains and found the Land poor and the woods very thick beyond them, Laurel & Ivy in and near the Branches."

"Our Horses suffered very much here for want of food. This day we came on the fresh track of 7 or 8 Indians, but could not overtake them."

"**April 27th**. We went [to the] remains of several Indian Cabbins and amongst them a round Hill made by Art about 20 feet high and 60 feet over the top."

Finding nothing but rough country unsuitable for Loyal Company claims, Walker turns back.

"A large Buck Elk killed Ambrose Powell's dog in the Chase, and we name the run Tumbler's Creek, the dog being of that name."

"**April 28th**. We kep up the River to our company whom we found all well."

Walker gave names, usually of the six men in his group, to all the streams they cross, and estimates their width. The purpose of his trip is to claim land: he is therefore meticulous about blazing trees and recording identifying marks.

"**30th**. I blazed a way from our house to the River. On the other side of the River a large elm cut down and barked about 20 feet and another standing just by it with the Bark cut around at the root and about 15 feet above. About 200 yards below this is a white hiccory barked about 16 feet. The bitten horse much mended, we set off and left the lame one. He is white branded on the near Buttock, and is old."

"**May 1st**. The Indian Road goes up the Creek, and I think it is that which goes through Cave Gap. 2nd. At the mouth of a Creek is a Lick, and I believe there was a hundred Buffaloes at it."

"**May 3rd**. We kep down to an Indian Camp, that had been built this Spring, and in it we took up our Quarters."

"**5th**. We got to Tomlinson's River. Plenty of Coal in the South Bank opposite to our Camp."

Walker notes "goslings," and concludes that "wild Geese stay here all the year."

"**9th**. Trees blown down about 2 years, obliged to go down a Creek to the River again, the Small Branches and mountains being impassable. 11th. Mountains very bad. Got to a Rock by the side of a Creek sufficient to shelter 200 men from Rain. Finding it so convenient, we concluded to stay and put our Elk skin in order for shoes and make them. May 12th. I have observed several mornings past, that the trees begin to drop just before day & continue dripping till almost Sun rise, as if it rained slowly."

"**14th**. When our Elks' skin was prepared we had lost every Awl that we brought out, and I made one with the Shank of an old Fishing hook, the other people made two of Horse Shoe Nailes, and with these we made our shoes or Moccosons. We wrote several of our Names with Coal under the Rock, & I wrote our names, the time of our comeing and leaving this place on paper and stuck it to the rock with Morter."

"**May 15th**. Laurel and Ivy increase upon us as we go up the Branch."

"**22nd**. To Milley's *[Kentucky]* River."

"**26th**. Our Dogs roused a large Buck Elk. He killed Ambrose Powell's dog in the Chase, and we name the run Tumbler's Creek, the dog being of that name."

"**31st**. We crossed 2 mountains and camped just by a Wolf's Den. They were very impudent and after they had been twice shot at, kept howling."

"**4th**. A very black cloud appearing, were just stretching a tent, when it began to rain and hail. A violent wind blew down our tent and a great many trees about it, several large ones within 30 yards of the tent. We all left the place in confusion and ran different ways for shelter. We met at the tent, and found all safe." ■

Gunpowder horn on elkskin, Cumberland Gap National Historical Park. The famous "Kentucky rifle" used blackpowder -- carbon and "saltpeter" (potassium nitrate or sodium nitrate). Most powder went into the barrel along with lead shot. A small amount of powder went into the "pan." When the trigger was pulled, a flint struck a steel plate creating a spark; the spark ignited gunpowder in the pan; the flame entered a small hole, igniting the main charge inside the rifle. For professional Long Hunters, Kentucky was "good business": they stayed in the woods for months at a time, returning with packhorses loaded with deer and elk hides, or buffalo, bear and beaver pelts. Some hides were sold for export. If hunters were at a "lick," hides might be cured with salt. Otherwise, they would be tanned in a shallow creek bed, using the tannic acid from chestnut and oak bark, and acorns.

Journal Excerpts, To Home

The return trip was rough, with "Laurel" and "Ivy" thickets almost impassable, and timber "being so blown down we could not get through."

"**June 6th**, 1750. Great sign of Indians on the Creek."

"**7th.** 12 miles to a river about 100 yards over, which we called Louisa River *[Tug Fork of The Big Sandy]*."

"**8th.** The River is so deep we cannot ford it. As it is falling we conclude to stay. Mr. Powell & myself were about a mile & a half from the Camp, and heard a gun just below us on the other side of the river. I was in hopes of getting some direction from the Person but could not find him."

"**11th**. It rained violently and the branch is impassable at present. We lost a Tomohawk and a Cann by the flood."

"**15th-16th**. Turkey are plenty and some Elks. We went a hunting & killed 3 turkeys. Hunted & killed 3 bears and some turkeys."

"**17th.** The Sabbath. We killed a large Buck Elk. 18th. Having prepared a good stock of meat, we left the Creek. The woods still continuing bad the weather hot and our horses so far spent, that we are all obliged to walk."

"**June 19th.** We got to Laurel Creek early this morning, and met so impudent a bull buffaloe that we were obliged to shoot him, or he would have been amongst us."

"**June 22nd.** Some large Savanna's. Many of the Branches are full of Laurel and Ivy. Deer and Bears are plentiful."

"**26th.** We crossed a Creek that we called Dismal Creek, the Banks being the worst and the Laurel the thickest I have seen."

"**28th.** Went down the Branch we lay on to the New River just below the mouth of Green Bryer. Powell, Tomlinson and myself striped, and went into the New River to try if we could wade over at any place. After some time having found a place we return'd to the others and took such things as would damage by Water on our Shoulders, and waded over leading our Horses. The bottom is very uneven, the Rocks slippery and the Current very strong."

Walker is now close to the edge of settlements.

"**July 6th**. We got on a large Creek which affords a great deal of very good land, and it is chiefly bought. We kept up the creek 4 miles and Camped. The creek took its name from an Indian called John Anthony, that frequently hunts in these Woods. There are some inhabitants on the Branches of the Green Bryer, but we missed their plantations."

"**July 7th**. 5 men overtook us and informed us we were only 8 miles from the inhabitants on a branch of James River called Jackson's River. We exchanged some tallow for Meal and Parted."

"**July 8th.** Having shaved, shifted, & made new shoes we left our useless Raggs at ye camp & got to Walter Johnston's about noon. We moved to Robert Armstrong's and staid there all night. The people here are very hospitable and would be better able to support travellers was it not for the great number of Indian Warriers, that frequently take what they want from them, much to their Prejudice."

"**July 9th.** We went to the hot Springs and found six Travellers there. The Spring Water is very clear and warmer than new Milk, and there is a spring of cold water within 20 feet of the warm one. I left one of my company this day."

"**10th.** We rode 20 miles & lodged at Captain Jemyson's below the Panther Gap. Two of my company went to a Smith and got their horses shod."

"**11th.** We travelled 30 miles to Augusta Court House *[Staunton]*, where I found Mr. Andrew Johnston, the first of my acquaintances I had seen since the 26th day of March."

"**12th.** Mr. Johnston lent me a fresh Horse ... About 8 o'clock I set off leaving all my company. It began to rain about 2 in the afternoon and I lodged at Captain David Lewis' about 34 miles from Augusta Court House."

"**13th. I got home about Noon.**" ■

Final entry in Walker's *Journal*: "We killed in the journey 13 buffaloes, 8 Elks, 53 Bears, 20 Deers, 4 Wild Geese, about 150 Turkeys, besides small game. We might have killed three times as much meat, if we had wanted it."

Wilderness Road or Ohio Flatboat?

Christopher Gist's 1751 exploration opened the Ohio river route into Kentucky, just as Dr. Thomas Walker's 1750 exploration opened the overland route.

Settlers from North Carolina and Virginia usually entered Kentucky via the Wilderness Road. Settlers from Pennsylvania and Maryland usually came down the Ohio in flatboats which could only float downstream. Some boats were large enough to carry families in cabins, with stables for livestock.

Journals **and maps of Gist and Walker provided essential geographical information about the western frontier.**

Land companies first had to obtain grants from Governors acting in the name of the British Crown. The next step was to "locate" and enter the grant, and prevail over hostile Indians, and aggressive French traders and soldiers.

France asserted sovereignty over Quebec and Canada and the entire Ohio-Mississippi valley to New Orleans. Britain did not accept French claims; the issue was not settled until the French and Indian War. Both competed for the profitable Indian trade -- valuable furs and beaver pelts exchanged for cheap "trade goods."

The Virginia Council acted to reaffirm the Colony's claim to the Ohio valley and create a buffer against French encroachment. In 1747, they granted The Ohio Company (prominent Tidewater Virginians such as Augustine Washington, George Mason, and Robert Carter) two hundred thousand acres between the Monongahela river in Pennsylvania and the Yadkin river in North Carolina.

The Company hired Christopher Gist, a trader and surveyor, as their envoy to the Indians and to learn about French intrusion. He was told to observe "Ways & Passes thro all the Mountains you cross, & take an exact account of the Soil, Quality, & Product of the Land, and the Wilderness & deepness of the Rivers & Mountains as near as you conveniently can. You are to draw as good Plan as you can of the Country You pass thro; You are to take an exact and particular *Journal* of all your Proceedings, and make a true Report to The Company."

Gist and a young black slave left Maryland October 1750. They "parleyed" in Kentucky with many Shawnee groups. Gist turned back when he was warned that hostile "French" Indians were camped at the Falls of the Ohio (*Louisville*) and he would be killed. Gist did not see Big Bone Lick or the Bluegrass. Returning via tributaries of the Kentucky river, they crossed trails used by Walker, reaching the Yadkin in May 1751. Mitchell's 1755 map relied on Gist's *journals*, and The Ohio Company asked him to represent them at the Treaty of Logstown, affirming their right to settle between the Allegheny river in Pennsylvania and the Ohio river.

In 1749 Celeron de Blainville came south from French Quebec to plant lead plates at the mouths of streams entering the Ohio. He also attached tin shields to trees along the way. Virginians viewed this as invasion. They were determined to eject the French, especially from the Forks of the Ohio [*present-day Pittsburgh*].

The man given the delicate task of warning off the French, was Major George Washington. In 1753, guided by Gist, Washington visited the French troops. He told them they were trespassing and must leave. The French were impressed with Washington: he was a fine figure of a man, six feet two inches tall, with strong features and an air of command. On the other hand, he was only twenty-one, his commission was in the Virginia militia, part-timers better known for drinking than fighting, and he had no soldiers with him. The French said they were staying.

In July 1755 Gist was principal guide for British General Braddock's ill-fated campaign against the French at Fort Duquesne. And from then until his death from smallpox in 1759, Gist used Indian scouts to guard the Virginia border. ■

16th Rain I made a Pair of Indian Shoes, those I brought out being bad

17th Still Rain. I went down the Creek a hunting and found that it runs into a River about a mile below our Camp. This which is Flat Creek and some others join'd, I called Cumberland River

18th Still Cloudy. We kept down the Creek to the River, and down the River along the Indian Road to where it Crossed. Indians have lived about this Ford Some years ago. we kept down on the South side. after Riding 5 miles from our Camp We left the River, it being very crooked. In Riding 3 miles we came on it again. it is about 60 or 70 yards wide. we Rode miles this day

19th Wee left the River but in four miles we came on it again at the Mouth of Licking Creek, which we went up and down another. In the Fork of Licking Creek is a Lick much used By Buffaloes and many

Dr. Thomas Walker's Journal, April 16-19, 1750. This portion of the Journal describes Walker's discovery and naming of the Cumberland River. The holograph *Journal* is in The Manuscript Division, Library of Congress, Washington, D.C.

How to Move the Line Farther West

Since the much-hated Proclamation forbidding settlement west of the Appalachians, the Loyal Company had been unable to control its grant of 800,000 acres of frontier lands. Settlers were warned off by the Proclamation itself. Two steps were required to make these lands available for settlement and speculation. It was necessary:

1) To quiet the claims of the various Indian tribes to this western territory; and

2) To move the boundary line farther westward. Dr. Thomas Walker achieved these aims for Virginia and for The Loyal Company.

When Sir William Johnson, Superintendent of Indian Affairs for the Northern Department, arranged for a great cession of territory to the Crown by the Six Nations, Walker's influence with the Virginia legislators was so strong he was able to secure the appointment, as Virginia's representatives at the Treaty of Fort Stanwix *[Rome, New York]* in October, 1768, of Andrew Lewis and himself -- the leaders, respectively, of the Greenbrier and Loyal Land Companies. As leaders of the Companies, the two commissioners had deep financial interest in having the boundary line moved farther westward.

> **By moving the boundary line west, Walker secured land for settlement while still appearing to adhere to the rule of law.**

A large territory south of the Ohio River and extending to the westward as far as the Tennessee River was ceded at Fort Stanwix by the Six Nations. Sir William Johnson also induced the Iroquois to sell an immense tract of land to a group of Pennsylvania speculators. (Johnson almost certainly received a "consideration" for this.) Walker, sensing the impropriety, reported to the Assembly that he signed as a witness, not as commissioner of Virginia.

The western boundary line of Virginia remained to be determined. But growing encroachments by white settlers on Indian territory and the steady pressure of population westward, made it urgent that a western boundary be established. The government in Williamsburg, the land companies and settlers had to know what land was, or was not, available for settlement and sale.

The Governor of Virginia arranged with John Stuart to run such a line. He negotiated a treaty with the Cherokee tribe at Hard Labor, South Carolina, on October 13, 1768, three weeks before the treaty at Fort Stanwix. The new boundary ran from Chiswell's Mine *[Wytheville, Virginia]* to the mouth of the Great Kanawha River.

When Walker and Lewis presented their report of the Fort Stanwix treaty, the Governor commissioned them to consult with Stuart in order to negotiate another line still farther to the west, in view of the recent cession to the Crown by the Six Nations of a vast territory at the back of Virginia.

The boundary line already agreed upon was still not satisfactory to the land companies. The treaty held at Lochaber, South Carolina October 18, 1770, established a new boundary, from the point where the North Carolina line terminates, due west to the Holston River, and thence in a straight line to the mouth of the Great Kanawha River. This line was run by Colonel John Donelson. By agreement with the Cherokee chiefs, for a consideration of four hundred pounds in addition to the original twenty-five hundred pounds, the line was changed to run from six miles east of the Long Island of Holston River direct to the Louisa River *[Tug Fork of the Big Sandy]* and down that stream to the Ohio.

Whether through an error, which seems inconceivable, or by collusion with the Cherokee chiefs, the line was run on to the Kentucky River, instead of only to the Louisa River, and thence down the Kentucky River to the Ohio.

By this maneuver, Virginia gained for nothing a much larger area. It was a great triumph for the land companies, especially the Loyal Company, since their grant was an area to the north and west of the southern boundary. *[Adapted from Henderson]* ■

The Dr. Thomas Walker-Cumberland River Historic Site is the "knob" rising above the confluence of Clear Creek, where Walker found and named the river.

Eighteenth-century surveying instruments in The Smithsonian Museum of American History: theodolite, Gunter's chain (22 yards, 100 links), compass and Jacob's staff, drafting instruments, chaining pins and flags. Surveyors were often the first Europeans into new frontier areas, and often claimed the most valuable land for themselves and friends.

Life, Liberty, & the Pursuit of Land

Thomas Walker was not born into Virginia's aristocracy. But thanks to a good marriage he acquired what it took to join their rank — an estate of several thousand acres — and added to it continuously. The gentry knew that *property* was the basis of the great fortunes of Mother England: land conferred status and power, and rank depended on the extent of one's property. The two

> **Every planter wanted more: more land, more wealth, more prestige. Just over the Blue Ridge were millions of acres, free for the taking.**

William Byrds, King Carter, and the James River tobacco-slave barons all had vast plantations; Lord Fairfax had title to six million acres. The pattern continued as settlement moved from Tidewater coastal plain, to The Fall Line, into The Piedmont. Sir William Berkeley, a 17th-century Governor, summed it up: "Westward the course of empire takes its way."

Tobacco is a labor-intensive crop. Indentured servants were the first workers, but their contracts lasted only seven years and many ran away. Slavery solved the labor problem: indentured immigrants declined after 1730.

Tobacco and primitive farming methods exhausted the soil, prompting a ceaseless demand for new fertile land. Every planter wanted more: more land, more wealth, more prestige. Just over the Blue Ridge were millions of acres,

Washington as a surveyor; "shingled" (overlapping) plats.

free for the taking. Speculative fever ran high. Virginians with political clout formed Companies to obtain from the Council vast grants of frontier land: The Ohio Company, Greenbrier Company, Mississippi Company, and Dismal Swamp Company. Boone's patron, Judge Richard Henderson, and his Transylvania Company followed the pattern: explore, survey, claim land beyond the mountains, lure settlers, sell plots to them, make a profit, acquire more land. Deeds were "flipped" often within weeks.

George Washington's compass and drafting tools.

Power was under the tight control of the wealthy. The Burgesses influenced the selection of Governors, and appointed the Council, judges, military officers and delegates to Federal conventions. There was a profitable web connecting families and land speculation. The Council and Assembly appointed Surveyors, such as Peter Jefferson, Joshua Fry, Walker, William Cabell, Andrew and Thomas Lewis, and William Preston -- and the County Clerks who recorded plats and titles. Appointments were made on the basis of political reliability. Land on the new western frontier was thus in the hands of those with the power to control grants, surveys, claims, and deeds.

Thomas Walker was a courageous explorer. He also knew how to draw surveys and maps advantageous to himself and his fellow-speculators in The Loyal Company. He did: and thus he and they profited. ∎

Historic reenactors at Colonial Williamsburg depict "Dr. Thomas Walker" presenting his map to the Virginia House of Burgesses, December 13, 1769. George Washington made a copy of this map, writing on the back, "Aligany/Copied from a Map of/Doct.r Walkers/laid before the Assembly." Washington used the map on a trip to the Little and Great Kanawha rivers beginning October 5, 1770 to claim land for veterans of the French and Indian War. Walker's map shows "Extent of ye Inhabitants 1769." This reference was intended to convince the legislators of the de facto settling of the western lands as far west as the Cedar River, and was thus part of the competition between The Loyal Company and The Ohio Company. The whereabouts of the original Walker map is unknown.

Albemarle Adventurers

Dr. Thomas Walker and his friends and neighbors, Peter Jefferson and Joshua Fry, were Members of The Loyal Company. Walker was Jefferson's physician, executor of his estate, and — for a brief time after the death of Peter — guardian of his son Thomas, who was later President of the United States. In setting out to explore The Loyal Company's grant in Kentucky, Walker's first stop was at the home of Colonel Joshua Fry.

These "Albemarle Adventurers" also proposed to explore the Missouri River and find a route to the Pacific Ocean. Their planning never came to fruition, but it is likely that the interests of this group in cartography, exploration, and western expansion were passed down, through family and personal relationships, to Thomas Jefferson and Meriwether Lewis, one of the principals in the Lewis and Clark Expedition.

Joshua Fry (1700-1754) was born in England, studied at Oxford, and was a professor of mathematics at William and Mary College. Around 1740 he became a planter on the Hardware River near Charlottesville. He was a justice of Albemarle County, along with Jefferson. He was also county magistrate, lieutenant, and surveyor. Because of his surveying experience, he was appointed to establish the boundaries of the Northern Neck, a grant of five million acres. Fry recommended that his friend Jefferson also be appointed, and the completed survey was approved by the Council in 1747. As a result, in 1749 Fry and Jefferson were appointed Virginia Commissioners to extend the boundary line between Virginia and North Carolina further westward.

In 1738, Joshua Fry petitioned the House of Burgesses for funds to produce a new map of Virginia; he was turned down four times. Finally, in 1750, the Board of Trade and Plantations in England authorized the governor to appoint "the most proper and best qualified" surveyors to complete a new map. Joshua Fry and Jefferson were commissioned to carry this out. They completed their map in 1751 and it was published in 1754 by Thomas Jefferys of London. In 1754 Fry, while serving as Virginia's top colonial military leader, died in a fall from his horse. His will left his surveying instruments to Jefferson.

Peter Jefferson (1708-1757) was of Welsh descent and a man of legendary size and strength. Though he lacked formal education, he was well-read and became a skilled surveyor and mapmaker. About 1735 he received a patent for 1,000 acres, and added 400 acres. Here he built his plantation Shadwell, where his son Thomas was born in 1743. He was one of the first residents of this frontier area. He became a justice of the peace, a county justice and sheriff, a lieutenant colonel in the militia, and represented his county in the House of Burgesses. In 1746 he and Thomas Lewis surveyed The Fairfax Line. Jefferson died in 1757. He left his surveying instruments and books to his son Thomas.

Only two copies remain of the first edition of the Fry-Jeferson map. It shows parts of the Middle Atlantic colonies from the coast to the Ohio River. It depicts the settled parts of Virginia very accurately and is the first map to show the Appalachians running in the correct direction.

A 1755 edition drew on data from George Washington, and others. That same year John Evans used this map (and data from Thomas Walker) in preparing his seminal "Map of the Middle British Colonies." Similarly, Gilles Robert de Vaugondy, geographer to the king of France, used a modified version of the map in his 1756 atlas. Both the British and French used the map in the French and Indian War and in the American Revolution. The map went through several editions, the last published in 1794. Thomas Jefferson used the Fry-Jefferson map in drawing his map for *Notes on the State of Virginia*. *[Adapted from Benson, III and 18.]* ■

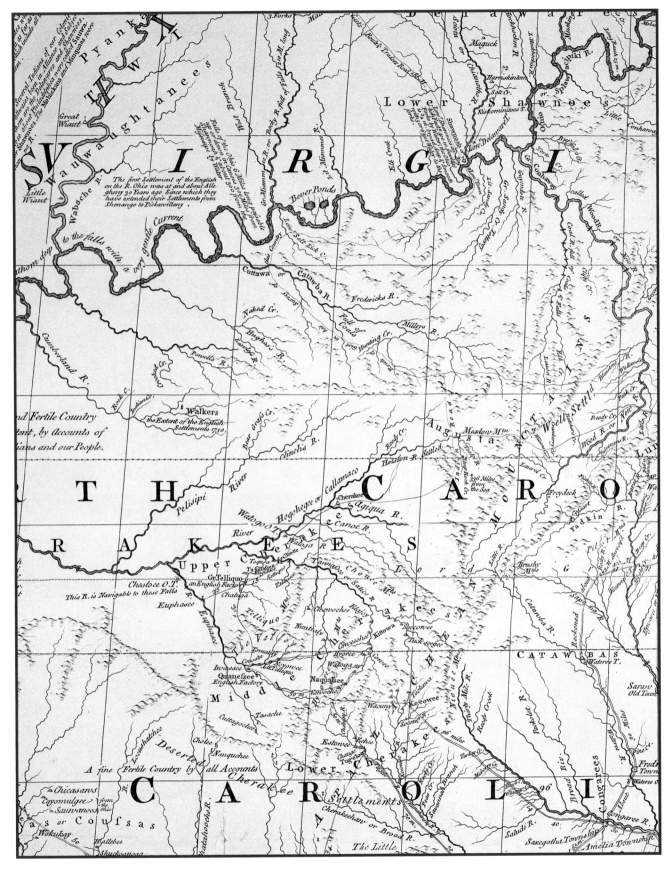

John Mitchell's famous map of North America (1755), drew from the journals of Christopher Gist in its representation of the Ohio Valley. The map also shows *"Walkers, the Extent of the English Settlements 1750."* Walker's tiny cabin is shown on a branch of the *"Cumberland R.,"* to the west of which is a large empty space, labelled *"A Fine Level and Fertile Country of great Extent, by Accounts of the Indians and our People."*

"Hawkeye" and Filson

Daniel Boone was born in Pennsylvania in 1734; his family later moved to the Yadkin Valley of North Carolina. Boone married Rebecca Bryan in 1756, but had little interest in farming or settled life. He much preferred hunting in unexplored areas west of the Blue Ridge. "*Something beyond the mountains always whispered*," as John Blakeless wrote. Boone had to see what lay beyond the ridge.

> **Boone followed the path Walker had used nineteen years earlier.**

In the winter of 1768-69, Boone's old comrade John Finley, showed up at Boone's cabin, full of fantastic tales of "Kentucky." Boone and Finley had met in 1758 during the battle of Fort Duquesne which included George Washington as aide-de-camp to General Braddock, and Thomas Walker as Commissary General of the Virginia Troops. Finley told Boone of huge buffalo herds feeding on great stands of cane, deer at every salt lick, lush land for the taking. Finley had also heard of an Indian path, an easy trail through the mountains. And so on May 1, 1769, Boone, Finley, and four others set out. They were gone two years.

They followed the route Walker used nineteen years earlier: Holston, Clinch and Powell Valleys to the white cliffs of Cumberland Mountain, then to Cave Gap. They followed the Warrior's Path to central Kentucky, and set up a base camp.

Boone tried to settle in Kentucky in 1773. But in Powell Valley, Boone's son James and his friend Henry Russell were captured by Indians and tortured to death. They were buried there. Boone and the would-be settlers turned back.

Two years later Boone joined forces with Richard Henderson, a North Carolina judge who organized The Transylvania Company, which Henderson intended to be the fourteenth Colony. His Company paid ten thousand pounds to Cherokee chiefs for 20 million acres between the Cumberland and Ohio rivers. On March 10, 1775, Boone and thirty men set out from Long Island *(Kingsport, Tennessee)* to clear a pack-horse "Trace." They followed the Warrior's Path as far as Flat Lick, then hacked through to open country in central Kentucky, where they built a stockade, Fort Boonesborough.

In 1778, the Fort was besieged for seven days by Shawnees led by British officers and Chief Blackfish. Later, on a salt-making expedition, Boone and 26 settlers were captured. Boone was taken to Old Chillicothe, where he was adopted by Blackfish and named *Sheltowee*, Big Turtle. Boone waited: when he learned that an attack on the fort was imminent, he slipped away from a hunting party, and covered the 160 miles to the fort in four days. The Fort survived another siege, interrupted by parleys with Indians.

In 1782, seventy Kentuckians were killed by a large group of Indians led by the infamous renegade Simon Girty in the Battle of lower Blue Licks, a western battle of The Revolution.

Like virtually everyone on the Kentucky frontier, Boone tried to make money speculating in land. But he was careless about filing claims and his efforts eventually came to naught.

Boone was brave in fighting hostile Indians, and a veteran frontiersman whose exploits were told and re-told. Over time, fact became myth, a myth exploited by John Filson, a speculator who hoped to lure settlers. Filson's book, *The Discovery, Settlement and present State of Kentucke* (1784) included the "Adventures of Col. Daniel Boon." The book led Europeans to see Boone as Rousseau's "natural man," and he was limned in Byron's epic poem, "*Don Juan*." James Fenimore Cooper used Boone for details of his character Natty Bumppo ["Hawkeye"] in "*The Leatherstocking Tales*." [*Faragher,* pp330-333] In 1799 Boone followed his son to Missouri. He continued to hunt and trap, dying in 1820, a few months shy of 86. ∎

The Kentucky Rifle was accurate. But one first had to load powder and lead shot into the muzzle, and prime the pan. Long Hunters and pioneers became quick and adept at this. The Kentucky Rifle was indispensable to settlers who used it to kill game for food. It was equally deadly against Indians and British troops during the Revolution.

My Old [Transylvania] Home

An ambitious and clever North Carolina Judge, Richard Henderson, would never be satisfied with mere acres! He dreamed of something much grander — an Empire. He, of course, would be its ruler. His plan was simple: gain control of all of Kentucky. Henderson's chief informant was Daniel Boone, who knew the area better than anyone. He was an expert hunter, and a brave and resourceful frontiersman. Kentucky was not the permanent home of any Indian group; it was, rather, a "game preserve" used by many tribes. After their defeat at Point Pleasant, WV in 1774 the Shawnees renounced claim to any land south of the Ohio, though they never intended to abandon their right to hunt there.

> **Kentucky was not the permanent home of any tribe; it was a "game preserve" used by many.**

The Royal Proclamation prohibited settlement west of the Appalachians as well as private land deals with Indians. Henderson ignored the decree. He challenged the "absurd doctrine of Kings and Popes having the right to claim and dispose of countries at their will and pleasure." He much preferred what he thought less absurd, that is, his having the same right.

With Shawnees defeated and out of the picture, the only Indians with any presence were the Cherokees — though they had no permanent settlements in Kentucky nor claims recognized by any group. On March 17, 1775, at Sycamore Shoals on the Watauga River (eastern Tennessee), the chiefs ceded all land north of the Cumberland and south of the Ohio between the mouths of the Kanawha and Tennessee rivers — virtually all of Kentucky, and large parts of West Virginia and northern Tennessee. The chiefs received trade goods worth ten thousand pounds. Henderson's Transylvania Company obtained a quit-claim to land it had <u>no right to buy</u> and the Cherokees <u>had no right to sell</u>. Governor Dunmore of Virginia, himself involved in speculative schemes, denounced Henderson's "infamous Company of Land Pyrates."

Chief Dragging Canoe took Boone by the hand: "Brother, we have given you a fine land, but it is a bloody ground, dark and difficult to settle." Boone, hired by Henderson, assembled 30 axemen, motivated by promises of land; he was to get two thousand acres. They went to work on March 17, 1775, and by April had cleared a "Trace" for pack-horses, forerunner of The Wilderness Road. After several bloody Indian attacks, they constructed a stockade, Fort Boone. Henderson followed with wagons, 40 pack-horses, and a herd of cattle. On the way, he met people fleeing the dangers of The Wilderness.

Henderson arrived at Boonesborough April 20. He drew plans for a stronger fort, but the axemen didn't want to work on it; their road contract had expired. They were eager to locate their land, build cabins, and start crops, as they had killed all the game in the area and food was scarce.

In May 1775, Kentucky's population may have approached three hundred persons, mainly in four settlements — Boiling Springs, Boonesborough, Harrodsburg, and Logan's Station. Henderson called for a civil government. Delegates met and provided for courts, a militia, the collection of debts, and the punishment of criminals.

In 1775 The Company sent an agent to the Continental Congress asking for equal footing with other Colonies. If this ploy had succeeded, Henderson would have become sole ruler of the Fourteenth Colony, the State of Transylvania. The matter was stalled by Virginia speculators unwilling to see valuable land slip through their fingers. On June 24, 1776, the Virginia Assembly declared: no land purchase may be made "from any Indian tribe or nation, without the approbation of the Virginia legislature." In November 1778, the Assembly declared Henderson's purchase void, though The Company was granted 200,000 acres as compensation for their settlement efforts. **Transylvania lasted just over three years.** ■

other, that I know of, except one about
to the North of it, which does not appear
as the other. The Mountain on the North
Gap is very Steep and Rocky. but on the
it is not so. We called it Steep Ridge.
ot of the hill on the North West Side
to a Branch, that made a great deal of
We kept down it 2 miles. Several other
coming in make it a large Creek, and
it Flat Creek. We camped on the Band
found Very good Coal. I did not se any
beyond this Ridge. we rode 13 miles

pt down the Creek 5 miles Chiefly along
Road

Sunday. Being in bad grounds for our
moved 7 miles along the Indian Road, to
ch. Clover and Hop Vines are plenty here

Portion of Dr. Thomas Walker's Journal, April 13, 1750. *This holograph version is included in "The William Cabell Rives Papers," Library of Congress, Washington, D.C.*

Win A War, Lose 13 Colonies

Poor farmers who wanted to settle the western frontier, and rich land company barons such as Thomas Walker who wanted to sell it, were delayed by the French and Indian War (1754-1763). The immediate issue was whether the upper Ohio Valley was part of the British Empire and therefore open to settlers from Virginia and Pennsylvania.

In 1749, the French ordered British colonists out, aiming to confine their settlements to land whose rivers ran east to the Atlantic. The Virginians moved to eject the French, claiming the area by treaty with the Iroquois, and Royal Charter.

> **Forbidding settlement of the western lands prompted widespread anger and united the colonists against English interference.**

George Washington had a big stake in The Ohio Company and stood to lose it if the French succeeded. So in 1754 he was chosen to lead "The Virginia Militia," a pickup group of untrained farmers, against Fort Duquesne (present-day Pittsburgh). They were soundly defeated.

In 1755 the British sent General Braddock and two regiments to oust the French, with Washington serving as one of Braddock's aides-de-camp, and Walker as Commissary General of the Virginia troops. This splendidly turned-out body of men — red coats, banners and drums — contrasted sharply with Washington's ragged militia, but they came to the same end. As Braddock's troops came up on Fort Duquesne, they were shot to pieces by a small legion of French troops who numbered perhaps one-fourth their number. With Braddock mortally wounded, and most of the officers dead or dying, Washington led the survivors back across the mountains.

Two decades after the engagement, Walker revisited the site and told a friend: "Braddock appeared to have courted defeat. Against every remonstrance of Major Washington and other officers, he refused to let a man leave his rank; they were shot down in whole ranks. The enemy, seeing the *infatuation* of the General, felt assured of victory, fired with such fatal precision as to cause our men to throw away their guns and run off in the greatest disorder. The officers attempted to arrest their course but were compelled to follow their example —without arms, the hellish yells of the Indians, and the groans and shrieks of the dying and the wounded falling upon their ears."

After 1757 the course of the war changed. British prime minister William Pitt saw a way to win by striking at Quebec, the heart of New France. On September 13, 1759, on the Plains of Abraham, both commanders, James Wolfe and the Marquis de Montcalm, were fatally wounded. Quebec surrendered, and a year later the whole of Canada had fallen.

By the Treaty of Paris (February 10, 1763) France relinquished all military and political power in North America. But the French defeat agitated the Indians who feared it would mean rapid expansion of English settlements. Pontiac, chief of the Ottawa, persuaded related tribes to join in an offensive against British outposts. The British, in a panic over Indian resentment and possible uprisings, issued the hated Proclamation decreeing that all land west of the Appalachians was an Indian Reserve, that colonial charters granted "sea to sea" (i.e., Atlantic to Pacific) did not apply west of this line, and that Indians, even if they wanted to, could not sell any of their homeland.

Forbidding settlement of the western lands prompted widespread anger — among colonists who wanted good land to farm, and among aristocrats who dreamed of yet more wealth to be made on the frontier.

Because the war had cost British taxpayers so much money, the King and his ministers concluded that the Colonies would have to pay their way, and passed Stamp Act duties. This insult to self-rule, and the fury caused by the hated Proclamation, led slowly, but inexorably, to the American Revolution. ■

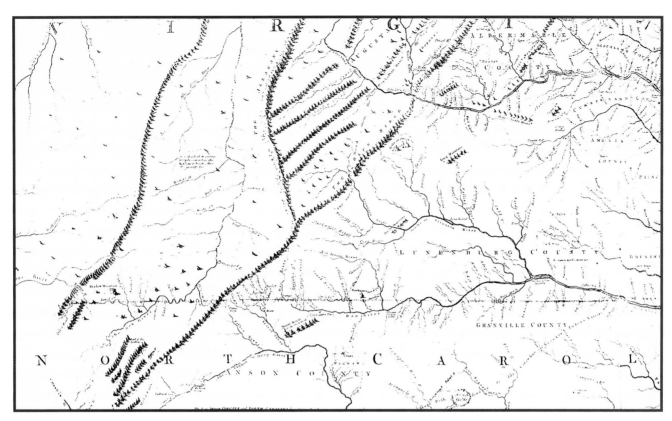

A portion of the map by Joshua Fry and Peter Jefferson (1751-54), showing parts of Virginia and the western "frontier." The "Louisa" river is shown in upper left.

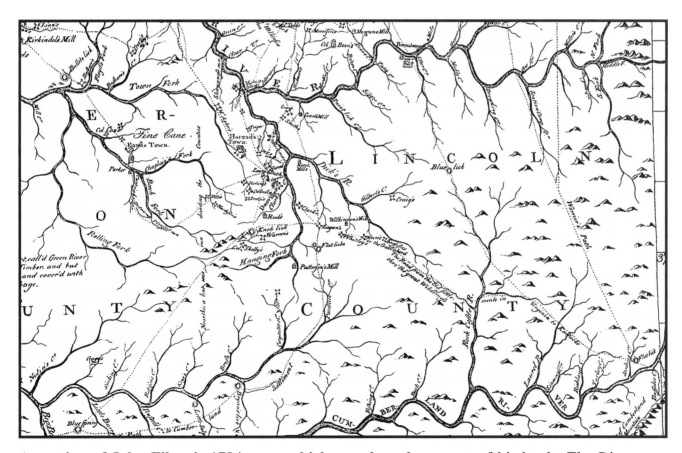

A portion of John Filson's 1784 map, which may have been part of his book, *The Discovery, Settlement and Present State of Kentucky.* Filson was a land speculator and shows areas of "Fine Cane," thought to indicate fertile soil, suitable for farming.

A Fat, Juicy Grant of Land

Up to 1754, the Governor and Council of Virginia gave away vast tracts of land -- 10,000 to 800,000 acres -- to individuals and groups organized as companies. The policy aimed, ostensibly, to attract settlers to the colony.

> *"When a fine old Virginia gentleman sets his teeth into a fat, juicy grant of land, he is extremely reluctant to let go."*

The main groups were The Loyal Company, The Ohio Company, and The Greenbrier Company. Their organizers are a veritable Who's Who of colonial Virginia: Lee, Taylor Washington, Dinwiddie, Mason, Carter, Fry, Nelson, Pendleton, Lewis, Walker, Jefferson, Maury, Meriwether, Willis, Henry, Mercer.

Magnificent lands in the "back parts of Virginia" were available at no cost to those with political and family influence. Walker, with his superior knowledge of the western country, was influential in organizing The Loyal Company, and his name appears second in the list of grantees after "John Lewis, Esq.," who immediately appointed him the Company's agent to explore and survey the western Wilderness.

The Company began to sell land as soon as Walker returned, and The Loyal Company issued hand-bills throughout the colonies inviting settlers to come and settle. The Company promised to survey the quantity of land they chose, at the cheap rate of three pounds per hundred acres. It also offered a time for payment, with the company to retain the title as security for the purchase money and to receive interest. Speculation fever ran rampant.

On June 14, 1753, the Council granted four years more to complete the surveying and selling. John Lewis gave up active leadership of the Company. He was succeeded by Walker, given the title of Agent. Except for the interruption of the French and Indian War, he was tireless in furthering the business of the Company until just before his death.

Population was streaming into southwest Virginia with many families "squatting" on back country land. Walker completed many surveys immediately and much land was sold, some to several hundred families already settled.

After the French and Indian War, the Company petitioned for a renewal of their grant, but were told the Colony of Virginia was limited by Royal Proclamation from "encouraging or any wise facilitating the settlement of the Western Frontier of the Colonies."

The Board of Trade said the purpose of the Proclamation was to confine the settlements to the coast so they might be "within reach of the trade and commerce of this kingdom" and be maintained "in due subordination to, and dependence upon, the mother country."

Walker and other land companies continued to survey and sell western land. This was the beginning in Virginia of revolt against British rule. The gentry were not much concerned with the Stamp Tax or tea -- but they were bound and determined to make money off land.

Leaders treated the Proclamation as a "scrap of paper." Washington derided it as a "temporary expedient to quiet the minds of the Indians," and sought to evade or circumvent it in any way possible. Mason mocked the "new fangled doctrine" of Indian claims and imperial control as a menace to colonial power. Jefferson's "Summary View of the Rights of British America" denounces as "fictious" the "principle that all lands belong originally to the king" and declares that the king "has no right to grant lands of himself." Henderson of North Carolina scoffed at the "absurd doctrine" that kings and popes had a right to dispose of land.

Southern rebels were determined to evade the King's control of "their" land.

Meanwhile, Walker was conniving with Cherokees to extend Virginia's boundary hundreds of miles to the West. *[Henderson, adapted]* ■

Cumberland Gap National Historic Park. The Wilderness Road might have looked much like this about 1800. Ruts might have been deeper — it was mostly hard going.

Pine Mountain Gap, a gorge carved through Pine Mountain by the Cumberland River. The digitally altered photo shows how the Gap might have looked in 1750.

The Gap was known to Indians as "Wasioto," and to Pioneers as The Great Pass or "The Narrows." Walker's *Journal* does not mention it: perhaps too obvious for comment.

Impelled by Fire and Spirit

Thomas Walker, born 1715, lost his father while still a lad and went to Williamsburg, Virginia to live with his sister, the wife of Dr. George Gilmer. Gilmer graduated from the University of Edinburgh, and was a physician, surgeon, and druggist. The young Walker lived in the drugstore, and his apprenticeship with Dr. Gilmer was his principal medical education.

> **Walker was connected by marriage, land speculation ventures, and politics to many of Virginia's most prominent citizens.**

Walker was a student at William and Mary College, but there is no record that he received a degree. Walker's medical license presumably came through Dr. Gilmer's representation that his student was well-prepared. Walker practiced medicine in Fredericksburg and eastern Virginia, and trained others. He won prominence as a physician and was described as "one of the most eminent surgeons in America." [Henderson, p82]

At the same time, he kept a general store in Fredericksburg, shipping hogsheads of tobacco to English and Scottish merchants in exchange for books, surveying instruments, medicines, and an amazing variety of English tools and cloth.

In 1741, he married Mildred Thornton Meriwether, a young widow. (Their daughter married Nicholas Lewis, uncle of Merriwether Lewis, co-leader of the Lewis and Clark expedition.) Through the marriage he acquired control of the Castle Hill estate, fifteen thousand acres in present-day Albemarle County. Managing a large estate and making it profitable required so much time that Walker began to abandon medicine, though he continued to treat a few friends, notably Peter Jefferson (father of Thomas Jefferson).

Like many "landed gentry" in Virginia, Walker learned surveying so as to subdivide his estate. He became quite skilled and was appointed Deputy Surveyor of Augusta County in 1752.

Walker was not tall, but he was a tough outdoorsman who loved hunting: one acquaintance called him "a wiry little blue-eyed man," while others noted his "fire and spirit."

Beginning in 1743, the Virginia Council, ostensibly to promote settlement of "empty" territories, began to make large grants of land to individuals and corporations. In 1745, the Council granted 100,000 acres to Colonel James Patton, and in 1748 Walker accompanied Patton as far as the Clinch River, to locate and survey the grant. Walker was said to have lived in the Wolf Hills area [today, Abingdon, Virginia] 1748-1754.

Given Walker's frontier experience and political and family connections, he was the logical choice to help lead the first of the "corporations." The Loyal Company was headed by John Lewis, who founded Staunton, Virginia. On July 12, 1748, according to Council records, a grant was made: *"To John Lewis Esq. & others eight hundred thousand acres in one or more surveys, beginning on the bounds between this colony and North Carolina, and running to the Westward and to the North, so as to include the said Quantity."* Others in The Company were Walker, several Meriwethers, Peter Jefferson and Joshua Fry. On December 12, 1749, Walker was appointed agent of The Company to explore the Western wilderness where the lands were to be taken up. He remained the most active member of The Company until his death in 1794.

We remember Walker today for his exploration of Kentucky in March-May 1750. But he served in many capacities over many decades. He had a hand in just about everything: Commissary General during the French and Indian War; representative in the House of Burgesses 1752-59 and 1761-71; and in the Assembly 1775, and later. He negotiated treaties with Indian tribes; was a cautious patriot (he had wealth to lose); represented Virginia in the survey to establish its boundary with North Carolina, and Tennessee and Kentucky. "A man for all regions," a frontier aristocrat, he travelled from New York to the Mississippi.■

Dr. Thomas Walker was a friend and physician to Peter Jefferson, and a partner with him in The Loyal Company. He was Executor of Peter Jefferson's estate and a guardian of his 14-year-old son, Thomas, for a brief period. This photo, in The Filson Club, Louisville, shows *The Papers of Thomas Jefferson*, opened to his first mention of Walker.

Limbs of The Walker Tree

Thomas Walker of King and Queen County, Virginia, married Susanna Peachy in 1707. Among their children was Thomas Walker.

Thomas Walker (1715-1794) married Mildred Thornton (1721-1778), widow of Nicholas Meriwether from whom she inherited a life-tenancy of several thousand acres in Albemarle County known as Castle Hill. She was distantly related to George Washington.

[There is no known portrait of Dr. Thomas Walker. A portrait by Saint-Memim, undated, was long thought to be of him, and a silhouette was produced from it. However, since Walker died in 1794 in his eighties, and the French artist did no work in this country until 1795 in New York City, the portrait of a young man could not possibly be of Dr. Walker.]

II: CHILDREN: Mary Walker (b. 1742), married Nicholas Lewis, uncle of Meriwether Lewis, Thomas Jefferson's secretary, and co-leader of the Lewis and Clark expedition.

Peachy Walker (b. 1767), married Joshua Fry II (1760-1839), grandson of Colonel Joshua Fry. Joshua Fry II was a member of the Virginia legislature before moving to Danville, KY.

III: GRANDCHILDREN: Among the children of Peachy Walker and Joshua Fry II was Martha Fry who married David Bell (d. 1847), and Lucy Fry, who married James Speed, scion of a family well-known in Kentucky politics.

IV: GREAT-GRANDCHILDREN: Among the children of Martha Fry and David Bell was Joshua Fry Bell (1811-1870). He graduated from Centre College, studied law at Transylvania University and practiced law in Danville. He served (1845-47) in the U.S. House of Representatives. During his service in the Kentucky House of Representatives (1863-67), he was responsible for the creation (1867) of the 112th county, named for him as Josh Bell County. The name was changed in 1872 to Bell County.

II: CHILDREN: Francis Walker (1764-1806) was a representative in the U.S. Congress from Orange and Albemarle Counties. He married Jane Byrd Nelson of York County. Their children included Judith Page Walker (1802-1882), who inherited Castle Hill.

III: GRANDCHILDREN: Judith Page Walker married William Cabell Rives (1793-1868). He studied law under Thomas Jefferson, served in the Virginia legislature and in the U.S. Senate for three terms, and was twice appointed Minister to France. Among their children was William Cabell Rives (1825-1890). His children include Dr. William C. Rives.

IV: GREAT-GRANDCHILDREN: Alfred Landon Rives married Sarah McMurdo. Among their children was Amelie Rives.

V: GREAT-GREAT-GRANDCHILDREN: Amelie Rives (1863-1945) "smoked, drank, and rode hard, and was considered very coarse in her day" [*Nyland p160*]; she was a novelist and playwright. She married a Russian portrait painter, Prince Pierre Troubetzkoy, and they lived in Castle Hill. ■

Clear Creek flows along the southern base of Pine Mountain before it joins The Cumberland River. The area now boasts a world-class golf course, a new addition to Pine Mountain State Resort Park. A mile farther up is Clear Creek Baptist Bible College, founded in 1923 to provide education for "mountain preachers" of the Gospel.

Talent, Energy, Land, Money

Trained as a physician, self-taught as a surveyor — Thomas Walker's life goal was neither of these, but money. He ran general stores in Fredericksburg and in Albemarle County, selling wheat locally, exporting hogsheads of tobacco and importing goods, such as sugar loaves, from Scotland and England. He owned and operated a saloon near Cobham, Virginia. He was a major stockholder in the Albemarle Furnace Company which worked mines along the Hardware River in the 1770s. He had an interest in an iron works, making pig and bar iron and castings.

In the larger scheme, however, these endeavors were side-shows: Walker's first entree to BIG wealth was through marriage to the wealthy 21-year old widow of Nicholas Meriwether who himself had inherited 1,650 acres in Albemarle County. Meriwether left his land to his infant daughter, born 1739 (the same year her father died), but Mildred, Nicholas' widow, retained life tenancy. Walker worked the land as though it were his own and in 1762 he bought the land for four hundred pounds and began building a substantial estate and gardens.

> To acquaint his son with the boundaries of his property, Walker took him one day to a tree in the woods where he gave him several blows with a horse-whip. When his son demanded to know "Why?" Walker replied, "My son, here is one of the corners of your estate, and I want you to remember it." Francis never forgot the boundary or the flogging.

In 1752, Walker was elected to the Virginia House of Burgesses, and was twice elected by two counties. He served in the House of Delegates, the Convention of 1775, the Committee of Safety, and the Executive Council. He was considered an expert on Indians, and represented Virginia at the Treaty of Fort Stanwix, and as a commissioner for Virginia and the Continental Congress at the Treaty of Fort Pitt. He led an expedition to establish the boundary between Virginia and North Carolina, and extended the line to Tennessee and Kentucky, and on to the Mississippi, where he located the site of a fort that became a basis for westward expansion.

Politics was interesting, but Walker's real passion was land and speculation. After 1750, he continued to explore, but land brought in more money. He became a wheeler-dealer — and he knew the right people: no other Virginian had as many connections among both Tidewater and Valley-Piedmont gentry. For several decades before and after the Revolution, he dominated western land speculation. He purchased adjacent tracts at his estate, Castle Hill, accumulating more than ten thousand acres, 86 slaves, 22 horses, and 93 cattle.

In May 1769, Walker was a member of the Assembly when Patrick Henry's declaration on the rights of the people was passed, in consequence of which Governor Botetourt dismissed the Assembly. Walker was among the patriots who re-assembled at a private house to form one of the first revolutionary conventions in Virginia.

In 1775, Walker, George Washington, Andrew Lewis, and other patriots met in a little church on a hill in Richmond to hear Henry speak:

"Is life so dear, or peace so sweet, as to be purchased at the price of chains and slavery? Forbid it, almighty God! I know not what course others may take; but as for me, give me liberty or give me death!"

Walker was considered "a patriot" — but cautious — with "a fortune at stake which could not be jeopardized by a political speculation."

After 1776, Walker was a commissary for troops and carried battle instructions to field commanders. He also saw a way to combine patriotism with money-making by buying a privateer vessel to raid British merchant boats. Why not help the war and make money at the same time? ∎

Pine Mountain State Resort Park offers many scenes that recall the earliest explorations of Kentucky -- by Dr. Thomas Walker, Christopher Gist, and Daniel Boone.

Harvest Of A Frontier Aristocrat

Thomas Walker is remembered because of his exploration of Kentucky. His *Journal* and maps located the Gateway, and settlers poured through.

But he did much more. His contemporaries respected his sharp intelligence and boundless energy. He was one of the most able, active, useful, and competent people in Virginia, or in any of the American colonies. He was a leader of men and of enterprises who inspired confidence. He served in many elected offices and on many Commissions, especially those dealing with boundaries and Indian affairs.

> **At his estate, Castle Hill, Thomas Walker welcomed five men who were either to be, or were actually at the time of their visits, Presidents of the United States**

He was a skilled physician and surveyor, as well as an expert hunter who knew Virginia's back country as well as any man. He was a resourceful and prosperous entrepreneur who managed a large plantation, adding and improving to it throughout his life.

He made his fortune as a supremely successful speculator on the western frontier of the colony. He was an organizer of The Loyal Company, its chief explorer and land scout, and served as its Agent until almost the day of his death in 1794. In old age, he appointed sub-agents and gave Powers of Attorney to his friends to collect money due the Company.

At Castle Hill, Thomas Walker lived the rich and colorful life of the Virginia aristocrat. At parties there, Jefferson played the violin and Madison danced. Walker welcomed five men who were either to be, or were actually at the time of their visits, Presidents of the United States, and many others who made their mark as statesmen, judges, diplomats, and soldiers.

The Company lived on after Walker's death, the original members pursuing their ownership through lawsuits prompted by conflicting claims, vague surveys, or ambiguous titles. In 1811 the last of the original members died. But their heirs continued to collect money due on land, and to institute suits. Francis Walker succeeded his father as Agent. The final suit was decided in 1871, 123 years after the original grant.

In his book of travels published in London in 1791, Thomas Anbury describes a visit to Col. John Walker, Thomas Walker's eldest son and Washington's aide-de-camp: "I was very much pleased with a very noble and animated speech of the Colonel's father, a man possessing all his faculties with strong understanding, though nearly eighty years of age. One day in chat, while each was delivering his sentiment on what would be the state of America a century hence, "the old man, with great fire and spirit, declared his opinion that the Americans would then reverence the resolution of their forefathers and would eagerly impress an adequate idea of the sacred value of freedom in the minds of their children, that it may descend to the latest posterity; that if, in any future ages, they should be again called forth to revenge public injuries to secure that freedom, they should adopt the same measures that secured it to them by their brave ancestors."

Archibald Henderson, author of a seminal article published by the American Antiquarian Society in 1931, describes his visit to Castle Hill, home of the famous Russian painter, Prince Pierre Troubetzkoy, and his wife, born Amelie Rives, "the noted writer," and great-great-granddaughter of Thomas Walker. "Two centuries meet here," Hendrson writes, in "singular conjunction architecturally."

Henderson describes Castle Hill as "one of the few houses now standing in Virginia erected before the Revolution." Walker's original building faces the mountains. Remodeled by William Cabell Rives in 1824, the nineteenth century house faces southeast with a generous portico supported on Corinthian columns and two conservatories stocked wtih native and exotic plants. ■

Castle Hill near Charlottesville. **Photo at top** shows the frame dwelling built in 1765 by Dr. Thomas Walker; it faced the mountains. In this house in 1781, Walker's wife delayed British Colonel Tarleton and his Legion so as give time for a warning to Jefferson and the Virginia legislators to escape the British plan to capture them. **The lower photo** is of the stately brick addition, facing east, erected 1823-24 by William Cabell Rives, minister to France, U.S. senator, and Confederate congressman. The estate is noted for tree boxwood.

Freedom and Independence = Land

The key to power and money in the eighteenth century was land. Lacking a hereditary noble class, this was even more true in colonial America than in England.

For settlers, "freedom" was land to farm. For speculators, "independence" was land to sell.

The original grant to the London Company of Virginia stretched to the "South Sea," and claiming this land drove much American exploration, as Friedenberg notes:

"'Greater Virginia' was the goal of repeated efforts, often led by Albemarle Adventurers, to explore beyond the Mississippi. Dr. Thomas Walker began planning in 1753. Jefferson urged in 1783 that George Rogers Clark find a route to the Pacific. In 1793, he promoted an exploration by Andre Michaux. His purchase of the vast Louisiana Territory and The Lewis and Clark Expedition (1803-1806) were the culmination of dreams which began at Jamestown."

The French, allied with the Indians, asserted that the land west of the Appalachians was theirs. This was the immediate cause of the French and Indian War, the North American phase of the global British-French "Seven Years War."

The Treaty of Paris ended the War, and an enormous territory many times the size of the seacoast colonies was up for grabs. The proudest English aristocrat and the most radical American libertarian were united in their passion to obtain this fertile western acreage. They were seemingly blocked by the British Proclamation which limited settlement to the eastern slopes of the Appalachians. The land west of the mountains was, in effect, the first Indian "reservation."

The land rush was based on the powerlessness of the Indians before the onslaught of masses of settlers moving westward -- and the desire of English lords and their colonial counterparts to enrich themselves.

There were also land squabbles. The Loyal Company, led by Dr. Thomas Walker and rooted in the Piedmont, competed with the Ohio Company, a Tidewater speculation in which the Washington family was prominent.

Sir William Johnson of New York, superintendent of Indian affairs for the northern colonies, used his connections with the Six Nations to enlarge his personal empire and also obtain land concessions for certain speculative companies.

The English lords had been fabulously successful in the 17th-century, treating the new continent like feudal fiefdoms: Sir Ferdinand Gorges received all of Maine; Sir William Alexander received Nova Scotia; Sir George Calvert picked up Maryland; when he was appointed governor of Virginia, Sir William Berkeley gave himself thousands of acres; his brother, Lord John Berkeley, was given western New Jersey; in 1673 Lords Culpeper and Arlington were given all of Virginia; and to settle debt and through the influence of his father, William Penn received Pennsylvania and Delaware.

The end of the French and Indian War seemed like a similar opportunity: the lords maneuvered within the government and forged alliances with powerful individual colonists. They aimed to obtain grants of land by gaining royal assent and by influencing the British Board of Trade.

The Proclamation was intended to thwart such schemes — but it was ignored by all. Poor white settlers streaming west viewed land companies with as much dread as they did Indians.

The English Privy Council saw unhindered settlement as insolence — disloyalty to Crown policy and a danger to British control of trade and manufacture. Tory colonists, stirred by traditional loyalties or too conservative to be swayed by political theories of French intellectuals, supported England. Those who did not support England claimed and settled as much land as they could — or laid low.

[Adapted from Friedenberg pp 17-103] ■

The Wilderness Road in Virginia, and after 1770 its extension into Kentucky -- "Boone's Trace" and "Scagg's Trace" — was suitable only for pack-horses, as shown in this photograph in Cumberland Ford *[Pineville, Kentucky]*. It was not until 1790 that "The Kentucky Road" was improved enough to be passable by wagons and stage-coaches.

Buzzel 'Bout Kentuck

When Louis XIV revoked the Edict of Nantes in 1685, he caused an outpouring of Protestants from Alsace. They fled into the German Palatinate along the Rhine River, where they received shelter. In 1708, an agent of William Penn visited the displaced German-speaking Alsatians and encouraged them to emigrate, describing the religious freedom in Penn's colony. By 1709, nearly 14,000 had come; they came to be called "Pennsylvania Dutch" (*Deutsch*). Many were mechanics, gunsmiths, shoemakers, paper-makers, butchers, blacksmiths, and ironworkers. They quickly found customers for their goods, such as the "Kentucky rifle" and Conestoga wagon.

> **English immigrants knew what they hoped to obtain in The New World — land!**

About the same time, families forced off their sheep crofts in Scotland, moved to Northern Ireland to establish the flax and linen trade. These people inhabited the poorest counties; they had few skills and many were illiterate. They were tenant farmers, and many were forced into debtor's prison by confiscatory taxes.

In addition, England controlled the wool and linen markets. English rule in Ireland was severe: as Presbyterians, the ex-Scots were persecuted both by Irish Catholics and the Church of England, who persuaded the government to punish any who spoke against their rule.

The final blow was famine, which struck in 1740. Starving, with no money and little hope, they grew desperate enough to brave the hazards of an ocean crossing, trusting they might find freedom and a new life in a New World.

The rigors of the Atlantic can hardly be imagined today. One vessel was seventeen weeks at sea. Sixty of its passengers died.

Those without money to pay their passage, were "bought" from the Captain, then herded by "soul-drivers" from town to town until someone hired them for a period of years. The soul-drivers and sea Captains got their money.

As one new immigrant wrote: "All the survivors are sick and feeble, and what is worst, poor and without means. When one is without money, his only resource is to sell himself for a term from three to eight years or more, and to serve as a slave. Families endure a great trial when they see a father purchased by one master, the mother by another, and each of the children by another. All this only for the money they owe the Captain."

English immigrants knew what they hoped to obtain in The New World — land! They were most often younger sons of farming families who, under the system of primogeniture, had no hope at all of inheriting any land, and no possible means of buying land. Their future looked bleak, and they dreamed of a better tomorrow. Some hired themselves out as laborers, or looked for employment in towns and cities. But the allure of The New World, an entire continent of fertile farmland, cheap or even free for the taking, was irresistible.

Other immigrants were refugees from brutal, seemingly-endless wars. They fled one conflict only to find themselves in the middle of another. *What kind of life is this?* They dreamed of security, a chance to make a success of farming, and raise their families in tranquility. As Harrison and Klotter note:

"What a buzzel is amongst people about Kentucke? To hear people speak of it one would think if was a new found paradise." An observer noted the migrants' crusading spirit. Ask these Pilgrims what they expect when they git to Kentucke. The Answer is land. Have you any? No, but I expect I can git it. Have you anything to pay for land? No. Did you ever see the Country? No, but Every Body says it is good land." [p 5]

Buoyed by faith, newly-arrived immigrants packed what they had and set off, following the rough Road over the Gap, venturing into an unknown "Wilderness." ∎

Settlers prized the fertile farmland of the Bluegrass prairie. Boone called it "A Great Meadow." The photo shows a hairpin bend in the Kentucky River with cattle and horse farms beyond. The earliest forts and settlements -- Harrodsburg and Boonesborough -- were located near this area of central Kentucky, the heart of Henderson's "Transylvania."

Kentucky: The Dream of Eden

Migration requires motivation: people will not otherwise pull up stakes and move. Frontier Kentucky was forged from the push of NEED and the pull of HOPE. In some cases the push was crop failure, religious persecution, or displacement by war. In other cases the push was depleted soil and slim prospects.

Kentucky exerted a magnetic, magical "pull" -- the allure of a dream, a vision, a hope. "Kentuck" evoked rich images. And hope was fanned by the schemes and hype of explorers, speculators, and land developers.

> **Flattering portraits of the new western land were aimed at promoting land sales to settlers and other speculators.**

For poor farmers seeking another chance, the western lands were a dream, a way to become free-holders and escape a bottled-up and declining East. Jefferson shared this image of agricultural paradise. In 1777 he outlined to the Virginia Assembly a plan to provide seventy-five acres in the new territory to each non-slave Virginia male after marriage, and allowed small farmers to buy up to four hundred acres at the county courts. Jefferson's vision was derailed by speculators who dramatically recast the law to serve their own profit. But his idea of a place where ordinary farmers could make a comfortable subsistence, fired the imaginations of many.

Prospective settlers had a belief — for some, a conviction — that beyond the mountains lay a land of bounteous promise. Elaborate descriptions circulated of a wild, exotic landscape of weird rock formations, beautiful flowering meadows, vast roaming herds of buffalo, medicinal rock springs, and restorative air.

Few descriptions equaled that of Felix Walker, Boone's companion during his trail-blazing trip in 1775. "A new sky and a strange earth seemed to be presented to our view. So rich a soil we had never seen before; covered with clover in full bloom, the woods were abounding in wild game — turkeys so numerous that it might be said they appeared but one flock, universally scattered in the woods. It appeared that nature, in the profusion of her bounty, had spread a feast for all that lives, both for the animal and the rational world. We felt ourselves to be passengers through a wilderness just arrived at the fields of Elysium, or at the garden where there was no forbidden fruit."

David Meade, a settler from Williamsburg, observed, "I have in view more Corn growing than all the crops which I may at Maycox put together for twenty Years would amount to."

Others spoke wondrously of the "amazing rapidity of the vegitation, or the immense powers of the soil." Letters back home urged friends and kin to "hurry on to Move to the Land of Milk & Honey, this almost paradise."

The visionary and idyllic note that was often struck in speaking about early Kentucky was not just poetic indulgence. Flattering portraits of the new western land were aimed at promoting land sales to settlers and investors. Nowhere did the romantic imagination and self-seeking profit motive merge more effectively than in the speculative land ventures that played such a large role in the settlement of Kentucky.

And no one played the land-grabbing game more ambitiously than Richard Henderson, a self-made lawyer and judge from Yadkin Valley in North Carolina. He dreamed of transforming the Kentucky wilds into the fourteenth Colony -- Transylvania. His scheme illuminates much of the hope, exploitation, and elusive promise that characterized the frontier. Henderson helped fund annual expeditions of Boone and other Long Hunters into the region -- advance men for his speculation. Henderson's scheme was clearly illegal: it violated the Proclamation that forbade colonial settlements west of the mountains; it trespassed on the rightful claims of Virginia and North Carolina; and it ignored the Crown's right of title to all undistributed lands. [*Smith, in Friend pp77-95*] ∎

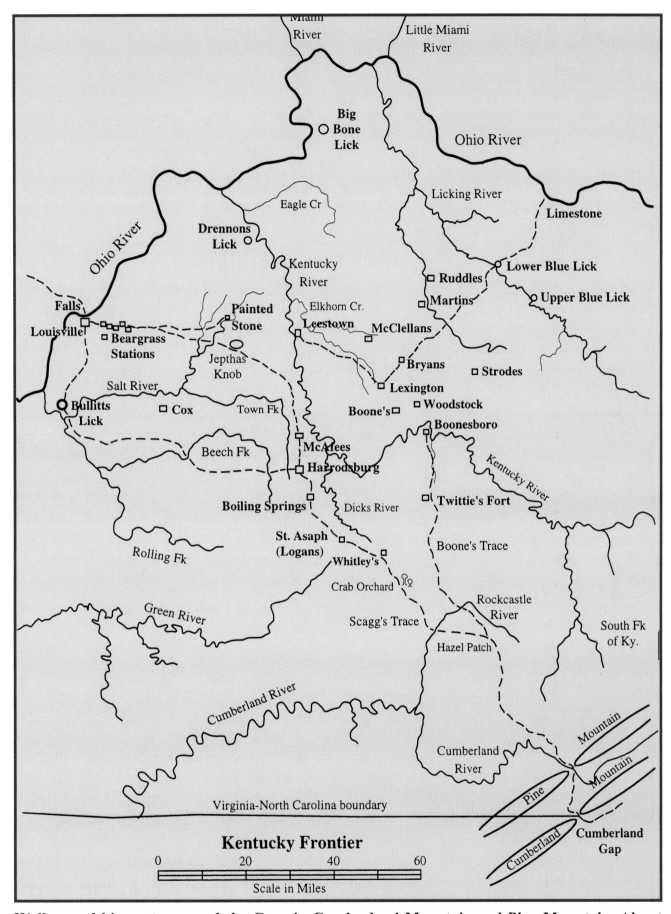

Little Miami
River

Miami
River

Big
Bone
Lick

Ohio River

Licking River

Eagle Cr

Limestone

Drennons
Lick

Ohio River

Kentucky
River

Lower Blue Lick

Ruddles

Upper Blue Lick

Martins

Falls

Elkhorn Cr.

Painted
Stone

Leestown

McClellans

Louisville

Beargrass
Stations

Jepthas
Knob

Bryans

Strodes

Salt River

Lexington

Woodstock

Bullitts
Lick

Cox

Town Fk

Boone's

Boonesboro

McAfees

Beech Fk

Kentucky River

Harrodsburg

Boiling Springs

Dicks River

Twittie's Fort

St. Asaph
(Logans)

Boone's Trace

Whitley's

Rolling Fk

Crab Orchard

Rockcastle
River

South Fk
of Ky.

Scagg's Trace

Green River

Hazel Patch

Cumberland River

Mountain

Mountain

Cumberland
River

Pine

Virginia-North Carolina boundary

Cumberland

Cumberland
Gap

Kentucky Frontier

0   20   40   60

Scale in Miles

Walker and his party crossed the Gaps in Cumberland Mountain and Pine Mountain. About twenty miles beyond Cumberland Ford, the group divided: three were left behind to build a cabin, while Walker and three others continued north about twenty miles. Walker climbed a tree; but seeing nothing ahead but yet more canebrakes and laurel thickets and no flat land suitable for farming (or land speculation), decided to turn back.

Kentucky: The Terror in Eden

The reality settlers found was not "Eden" but deprivation, and constant fear of Indian attack. A keelboat came floating down the Ohio, "every person on it dead," Benjamin Allen remembered. "Found an Indian's fingers that had been chopped off," presumably while trying to climb in.

Scores fled the terror. Richard Henderson passed a hundred heading back, some returning for their families, but most running from the Shawnee. Their fears frightened everyone. "The general panic that had seized the men ...was contagious; it ran like wildfire."

> **Indians often destroyed crops, despite efforts by settlers to poison them by leaving crops impregnated with Arsenic.**

Settlers crowded into the forts, usually little more than a stockade. The hastily-built cabins were of logs, one story high, thirty feet by sixteen feet, one door, no windows, a half-finished chimney. Corn could be planted or tended only with great danger. Boone had to divide the men at Boonesborough, one group to protect the group trying to plant. Even so, Indians often destroyed crops, despite efforts by settlers to poison them by leaving crops "impregnated with Arsenic." Indians frequently made off with the settlers' horses -- about two hundred were reportedly stolen in the spring of 1777 alone.

A minister in Harrodsburg in 1776 described the stark realities of the western frontier: "A poor town. A row or two of smoky cabins, dirty women, men with greasy hunting shirts, leggings and moccasins. I there ate some of the first corn raised in the country, but little of it, as they had a very poor way to make it unto meal; we learnt to eat wild meat, without bread or salt."

Josiah Collins, reaching Boonesborough in March, 1778 observed: "We found a poor distressed 1/2 naked, 1/2 starved people; daily surrounded by savages, so dangerous, the hunters were afraid to go out to get buffalo meat. Whole families are destroyed without regard to age or sex; infants are torn from their mothers arms and their brains dashed out against trees. Not a week passes, and some weeks scarcely a day, without some of our distressed inhabitants feeling the fatal effects of the internal rage and fury of these execrable hell-hounds."

One woman said: "if the men went out, they were sure to be killed; & had therefore to lay still." John Floyd wrote the governor of Virginia in 1781, "We are all obliged to live in our forts, and notwithstanding all the caution we use, forty seven killed or taken prisoners by the savages, besides a number wounded, since January." The year before, "Hardly one week pass without some one being scalped between this [place] and the Falls and I almost got too cowardly to travell about the woods without company."

No place, no moment, was safe. Daniel Drake recalled a 1791 wedding in Mayslick that was halted because of an impending attack. "Indian wars, midnight butcheries, captivities and horse stealings, were daily topics of conversation." Parents and children witnessed one another's torture and death. In December 1790 Benjamin Allen and his father were caught at Mud Lick Branch. Benjamin was sixteen. Indians captured him, while they killed and scalped his father. The boy later saw his father's scalp "stretched on a hickory hoop at the camp."

Joseph Mitchell was coming down the Ohio in 1788 when Shawnees stopped his boat, boarded it, and beat up several men. Mitchell's son "was burnt before his eyes."

One woman saw her husband killed by Indians in her home, along with all but two of her children. "Mrs. Davis had gone out in the night to bring in some clothes. Saw the Indians go in the cabin and kill her husband, and into the kitchen and kill all the negroes ...The Indians took four children, two boys and two girls, and sold them to the french." [*Adapted from Smith, in Friend, pp77-95*] ∎

The Gap in Cumberland Mountain was first used by animals, then by Indians, then by Long Hunters, who called it "Cave Gap" because of the cave *[later called "Cudjo's Cave"]* whose entrance is just below the top of the saddle. Dr. Thomas Walker passed through the Gap in 1750, and described it in *The Journal* of his exploration of Kentucky, March-July 1750. Between 1775 and 1810, about 300,000 pioneering men and women passed through. The area is today the site of Cumberland Gap National Historical Park. A portion of "The Wilderness Road" is being restored to the way it would have looked almost two centuries ago. [Copper engraving by H. Fenn, published by D. Appleton & Co., New York, 1872.]

Make A World Out of Chaos

The Great Meadow is the classic novel about the settlement of Kentucky. It is also about the *idea* of Kentucky, the New Eden over the mountains. It is among the most enduring work of Elizabeth Madox Roberts (1881-1941).

The story is told through the eyes of Diony Hall. Her father was a lover of books and a disciple of the English idealist Berkeley. He imparts a great deal of philosophy. Diony also masters the skills of pioneer women — how to grow and preserve food, shear sheep and spin and dye wool thread, how to make linen thread and cloth. And be strong, make do, do without.

> *"It must be a great content to a man to go into a new country and name there the rivers with names he would fancy."*

She remembers the arrival of a neighbor: "He told of a surveyor he had met on the trail who had been far into the continent beyond the mountains and down into the valleys. I never before in all my time heard tell of a land so smooth and good. He said a buffalo road goes north and south through the land, where the beasts go to salt themselves at the great licks. Cane upwards to twelve feet high. The soil rich like cream. Fat bears, the fattest he ever did see, he said. A prime place to fatten hogs."

"But between here and there are a power of rough mountains. How are these mountains named, that you tell of? He said they were the Ou-as-i-o-tos. *Ou-as-i-o-tos* -- all saying it, trying the syllables on their lips."

Later an old hunter tells of the river valleys: "There is first the Tenn-ess-ee, the farthest water. Then, moving hitherward, you would come to the Shawnee River, and this has been called — it is a pity — has been sometimes called the Cumberland. Meadow and woodland as far as eye can behold. Beauteous tracts in a great scope, miles. To the east is a boundary of rugged mountains. A great wall stands across the way. But high up, cut in the cliff, is a gate. I was in and out of it for years to peer out the land and spy its wonders."

"I walked far. All the fore part of one year and on until summer came I hunted beyond the Chenoa River. Cho-na-no-no. Some say Cuttawa. Some call it Louisa and call the land the same. Some call it Kentuck. Wild plum in flower in the spring-o'-the-year. Peavine, nettle, rich weed. Timber a fair sight to see. Honey-locust, black walnut, sugar tree, ironwood, hoopwood, mulberry, elm. Oak a-plenty. Ash trees fifty feet high. Game everywhere. Waterfowls, otters, beavers, turkeys, elk, deer. You could never hunt your fill. Pigeons black the air and their flights are like a thunder in the sky. A new world has begun in that place. It is a long way, but the reward is more than labor. A land of beauty, a garden place. But a weary road through the wilderness. No path under foot, and savages to kill you and get your skulp maybe."

Diony and Berk Jarvis are married and follow The Wilderness Road. The novel never minimizes the dangers, including Indian attacks and torture and death, the rigors of Harrod's Fort, clearing forest, and breaking new ground. But beyond dreams of fertile land and "a fine high house," Diony and other "civilizers" would "make a world out of chaos." "It must be a great content to a man to go into a new country and name there the rivers with names he would fancy. To name a river and write it on a map." Her father says: "For such a length of time as it staggers the mind to contemplate, Man has been marching outward. Kentucky will breed up a race of heroes, men built and knitted together to endure, a new race for the earth."

> **Diony's migration and that of thousands of others** takes place during the Revolution, 1774-1781. While battles in Virginia and Massachusetts brought political independence this poetic novel suggests the democratic spirit of the country sprang from the challenges of the frontier itself.
>
> *[Adapted from Roberts, 1930]*

Walker's *Journal* notes the spring and cool air flowing out of Cudjo's Cave, in the saddle of Cumberland Gap. He said the stream of water was sufficient to turn a Mill.

Daring Raids to Save the Settlements

Dr. Thomas Walker showed The Way West. But migration was delayed by the French and Indian War which caused most of the tribes to shift their allegiance from the French to the British. By 1777 the British at Detroit were sending Indian war parties to attack settlers.

Every Kentucky "station" was raided. Settlers endured ambush attacks and scalpings. There was panic and desperation in the forts.

George Rogers Clark (1752-1818), a tall red-haired man with much frontier experience, assumed leadership of the settlers. His efforts led to the establishment, December 31, 1776 of "Kentucky County" as part of Virginia — and ended Henderson's Transylvania scheme.

Clark was a skilled and fearless fighter who argued that Kentucky could be saved — but only by striking Indians (and their British supporters) in their home base. A magnetic leader and persuasive orator, he petitioned Virginia's Governor, Patrick Henry, for authority to raise troops and money. Clark was commissioned a Lieutenant Colonel, and given secret orders to attack British posts. He recruited his "Expeditionary Force" — 150 frontiersmen, all expert in survival — by offering 300 acres of land. They set out from the Falls of the Ohio *[Louisville]* on June 24, 1778. Clark's raids resulted in victories at Kaskaskia and Cahokia.

He went on to take Vincennes, Indiana. British Governor Henry Hamilton [called "The Hair Buyer," because he allegedly paid Indians for American scalps], based in Fort Detroit, assembled a force of regular troops, volunteers and militia, artillery, and Indian warriors. He marched to Vincennes, re-taking the fort in mid-December 1778. But he unwisely chose to wait until Spring before confronting Clark, and allowed most of his forces to return to their homes for the winter.

Statue and mural, George Rogers Clark National Historical Park, Vincennes, Indiana

Clark re-grouped at Kaskaskia, then led 170 Virginians and Illinois French volunteers on an incredible 18-day march across present-day southern Illinois. The Wabash was flooded; often in freezing water up to their shoulders, Clark's leadership and laughter brought them through. It was a brilliant masterpiece of military strategy. Clark said the British "could not suppose that we should be so mad as to attempt to march 80 Leagues through a Drownded Cuntrey in the Debth of Wintor."

Upon reaching Vincennes, Clark attacked immediately, unfurling militia flags suggesting a much larger force, and tunneling toward the fort. Four Indians caught carrying American scalps were tomahawked to death in full view of the defenders of the fort. Hamilton surrendered, and the American flag was raised February 25, 1779.

Clark's victories prevented the British from driving Americans from the frontier. He added to the United States a rich area as large as the original thirteen colonies.

Indian terror was reduced and settlers moved West again. But the Indians were not through. In the summer of 1782 Shawnees and others decided to eliminate the Kentucky settlements while British help was still available.

On August 19, 1782 at lower Blue Licks (the last "western" battle of the Revolution) 70 Kentuckians were killed and 20 others captured. The defeat led to fury and recrimination among the settlers. Clark had not been near the battle — but he was blamed by militia officers. Clark led a retaliatory raid against the Shawnee, but it was not enough. The Hero of Vincennes became the scapegoat for a frontier defeat. ■

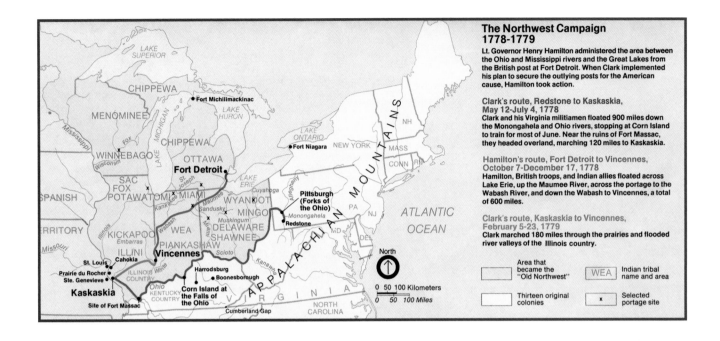

The Northwest Campaign 1778-1779

Lt. Governor Henry Hamilton administered the area between the Ohio and Mississippi rivers and the Great Lakes from the British post at Fort Detroit. When Clark implemented his plan to secure the outlying posts for the American cause, Hamilton took action.

Clark's route, Redstone to Kaskaskia, May 12-July 4, 1778
Clark and his Virginia militiamen floated 900 miles down the Monongahela and Ohio rivers, stopping at Corn Island to train for most of June. Near the ruins of Fort Massac, they headed overland, marching 120 miles to Kaskaskia.

Hamilton's route, Fort Detroit to Vincennes, October 7-December 17, 1778
Hamilton, British troops, and Indian allies floated across Lake Erie, up the Maumee River, across the portage to the Wabash River, and down the Wabash to Vincennes, a total of 600 miles.

Clark's route, Kaskaskia to Vincennes, February 5-23, 1779
Clark marched 180 miles through the prairies and flooded river valleys of the Illinois country.

Area that became the "Old Northwest"	**WEA** Indian tribal name and area
Thirteen original colonies	**x** Selected portage site

Cover: *The Surrender of Fort Sackville, February 25, 1779, by H. Charles McBarron.*

Courtesy Department of Defense, Washington, D.C.

Clark was an audacious and successful commander of the American Revolution in the West. His victories gained much territory for the new nation.

Isaac Shelby and Cumberland Ford

Isaac Shelby, elected governor when Kentucky became a state in 1792, was a hero of The American Revolution. Born in Maryland in 1750, he moved in 1772 to the Holston valley, and served in both the Virginia and North Carolina legislatures. He was a surveyor in western Virginia and North Carolina, for himself and for the Transylvania Company.

He told friends he had been with Dr. Thomas Walker in 1770 on Yellow Creek, and that Walker told him of having been on Cumberland Gap twenty years earlier.

> **Shelby owned land near Cumberland Ford, where the Kentucky Road crossed.**

Indian Fighter

Shawnees felt their claim to hunting grounds in Kentucky had been ignored in the 1768 Treaties of Hard Labor and Fort Stanwix, slighted both by whites and by Cherokees and Iroquois. Shawnees began deadly attacks on Kentucky settlements, and Virginia Governor Dunmore resolved to break their power. "Westerners" eager to open Indian lands to settlement — including George Rogers Clark and Isaac Shelby — rushed to "Lord Dunmore's War." Shelby had a massive, imposing build and a reputation as a fierce Indian fighter. The Shawnees, led by Chief Cornstalk, were defeated October 10, 1774 at Point Pleasant, where the Kanawha River joins the Ohio.

Revolutionary War

The Carolinas were home to many wealthy Tories, loyal to Britain; the Revolution there was largely a civil war. British Colonel Tarleton and his elite Legion demolished Abraham Buford's Virginia Regiment, sent by Washington to help South Carolina patriots.

In 1780, Shelby, now a Colonel of militia, arrived at the head of 200 horsemen, mostly mountaineers from the Watauga, Nolachucky and Holston settlements of North Carolina. They were armed with accurate muzzle-loading "squirrel rifles." Shelby, along with a detachment of Georgians, inflicted hard blows against the British at Musgrove Mill. The British put out a reward for him "dead or alive."

Men from North Carolina and Tennessee led by Shelby, and men from Kentucky and Virginia, attacked a strong British-Tory position at King's Mountain, South Carolina. They scaled the steep cliffs and made the woods ring with Indian war-whoops. A thousand Tories were killed, wounded, or captured; the patriots lost only 28 killed. This was the turning point of the war in the South, and led to victories at Cowpens and Guilford Courthouse, and to Cornwallis' surrender at Yorktown October 19, 1781.

Ford Owner

Shelby settled near Danville, KY and owned land, a house, and a ferry at Cumberland Ford.

In the middle of the Ford was a sandstone boulder, a foot above the water at its fordable stage. This served as a water-gauge: if the boulder could be seen, the River could, with care, be safely crossed. When the boulder was under water, the traveler had to camp for awhile.

In 1797 the Legislature appropriated five hundred pounds "for repair of `The Wilderness Road' at `The Narrows' [Pine Mountain Gap]." [The Wilderness Road had three choke-points: Cumberland Gap, "The Narrows," and Cumberland Ford.] A toll-gate was built at "The Narrows" and stayed there until 1830, when it was moved to the Ford. It remained until 1865.

Lush bluegrass made Kentucky a big livestock producer: cattle, horses and mules moved in large numbers to eastern markets. Toll-gate receipts for 1827 show 111,823 hogs herded along in one year.

The village grew up alongside The Road. The Ford, like Cumberland Gap, was of strategic importance in The Civil War, occupied first by Confederate then Union troops. Remains of breastwork trenches can still be seen. ■

Cumberland Ford *[Pineville, Kentucky]* is noted on Tanner's map of 1839 and Black's map of 1867. It was a crucial part of The Wilderness Road, being the only place where the river could be forded easily. The Toll-Gate was located here after 1830.

Fat Hens Paid the Toll

From a letter to *Kentucky Exlporer* by Dora DeHart, June 1995:

"The article about tollgates was of great interest: my husband's g.g.g.g.grand-father, Dillion Asher (1777-1844), was one of the first operators of The Wilderness Road tollgate." [The first was Joseph Crocket (*sic*); the gate was first located in The Narrows (Pine Mountain Gap); the village of Cumberland Ford ("Old Pineville") grew up around the gate and the keeper's house].Between 1775 and 1800 about 200,000 people passed through. When Kentucky became a state in 1792, people saw the need for a way to pay for the upkeep of The Road."

> **Law-makers never considered that many people coming through had no money of any kind.**

"The state was to receive all the fees collected, but there were many kinds of money including foreign money. Pretty heated discussion sometimes resulted. This went on until the legislature passed a bill that fees had to paid in U.S. coins."

"The law still had flaws. The law-makers never considered that many people coming through had no money of any kind. Travelers were prepared to pay, but had no money. They paid their toll with things like fat hens, bushels of apples, baskets of vegetables, sometimes livestock, whatever they could do without. Now what was the tollgate keeper to do? Rush all this stuff to Frankfort?"

"My guess is that Dillion paid the State cash out of his pocket, but made a little bonus. How could people in Frankfort put a price on commodities so many miles away? That's how tollgate keepers got a bad reputation. Most of them were considered wealthy. Dillion Asher was not a wealthy man but made a good living after the tollgate days in logging and timber. His cabin was built before 1800 and still stands on Red Bird River where he raised his family. He died there and is buried on the hill above the house. The Kentucky Historical Society declared the home an Historic Site, and it is now a tourist attraction. Dillion's descendants willed land for a school, so children could get the education they would otherwise have been denied." ■

For more than two hundred years Cumberland Gap has been a great key to Kentucky for travelers coming from Virginia and North Carolina. It provided a path used by uncounted legions of immigrants who spread across the commonwealth and into the west. This view was sketched on the eastern side of the tollhouse that was part of any turnpike constructed by a road company.

Wood engraving from Bryant's *Picturesque America*, 1873, from a drawing by Harry Penn. The same view appeared in *Appleton's Journal*, March 16, 1872.

ACT FOR A ROAD TO THE GAP

"The keeper of the turnpike shall be entitled to receive the following toll: each person, except post riders, expresses and women and children under the age of ten years, nine-pence; every horse, mare or mule, nine-pence; every carriage with two wheels, three shillings; every carriage with four wheels, six shillings; every head of meat cattle going eastward, three pence. Each head of hogs 1/2 cent; each head of sheep 1/5 cent; each vehicle drawn by one horse or mule, 20 cents; each wagon drawn by three horses, mules, or oxen, 30 cents; each stage coach with seats inside for six passengers, 35 cents."

Fog-filled valley and mountains in autumn, Pine Mountain State Resort Park, KY.

Dillion Asher, one of the first Toll-Gate Keepers on The Wilderness Road, constructed this cabin before 1800 at Red Bird, in Bell County, Kentucky. His descendants gave land for The Red Bird Settlement School and Hospital, which continues to serve the remote area.

"Not Even Jack-Assable"

Dr. Thomas Walker's exploration of the unknown interior beyond the mountains — a green wilderness said to be filled with game, lush meadows, and immense herds of buffalo — began with a fairly easy jaunt down the Valley of Virginia. The Great Wagon Road follows this broad natural "boulevard" of great beauty and rich history.

> **Today, the old Wilderness Road is four lanes wide and 70 miles per hour all the way.**

Settlers moved along The Road from the early 1700s. Southbound traffic numbered tens of thousands of people a year; it was the most heavily travelled road in all America. Joshua Fry and Peter Jefferson's 1751 map of Virginia calls it "The Great Wagon Road from the Yadkin River through to Philadelphia distant 435 miles."

The Road carried the ancestors of **John Sevier** of Tennessee, **John Calhoun** of South Carolina, **Sam Houston** of Texas, **Cyrus McCormick** of Virginia, **Henry Clay**, and **Abraham Lincoln**. The procession began with hunters, Indian traders, soldiers, missionaries, peddlers, and farm families hoping to clear land and make a crop. **Davy Crockett** knew it as an explorer; **George Washington** as surveyor and frontier militia officer. **Andrew Jackson, Francis Marion, Lighthorse Harry Lee,** and **Daniel Morgan** moved troops along it.

When British forces captured Philadelphia, the Continental Congress fled down the Wagon Road to York. **Cornwallis** and his Redcoats traveled the Road, and important battles of the Revolution — Kings Mountain, the Cowpens, Guilford Courthouse — were fought near it.

Many towns owe their beginnings to early campsites along the Road. Some grew up around a tavern or inn, a ferry or ford, or a county seat, later becoming a center of farming and industry. The route ran from Philadelphia, a main port for immigrants, to Lancaster, York, Gettysburg, Harper's Ferry, Staunton, Lexington, Winston-Salem, Salisbury, and Charlotte.

At "Big Lick" *[Roanoke]*, the Road forked to the Carolinas, or via Abingdon to The Wilderness Road, to Knoxville and Nashville, or via Holston, Clinch and Powell valleys to the gaps in the Cumberland and Pine mountains, and Scagg's Trace or Boone's Trace to central Kentucky.

The Road was not easy: rain brought mudholes, summer drought dust-bowls. Winter was worst of all. As one local ditty put it:

> *"I say it's not passable,*
> *Not even jack-assable,*
> *And those who would travel it*
> *Should get out and gravel it."*

Toll-gates, as at Cumberland Ford, generated income for maintenance. But poor farmers could not understand why they were expected to PAY

NOTICE TO GATEKEEPER

We ast you not to collect no more tole, you must Not collect one cent if you do we are Going to Destroy your House with fire are Denamite So you must Not collect No more tole at all. We don't want to do this but we want a Free Road and are agoing to have it, if we have to kill and burn up everything. Collect no more tole we mean what we say, so Fair warning.

(!) to get their harvests and cattle to market.

Pack-trains, freight wagons and stage coaches (which also carried the mail) continued down the road to the Civil War. Canals began moving bulky goods in the 1820's and 1830's, however, and railroads took over after 1850. Today, of course, the "great wagon road" is four-lanes and 70 mph all the way. The people who traveled this Road worked hard, faced terrible enemies, and usually died young. But they left us a great, free nation.

[Adapted from Rouse] ∎

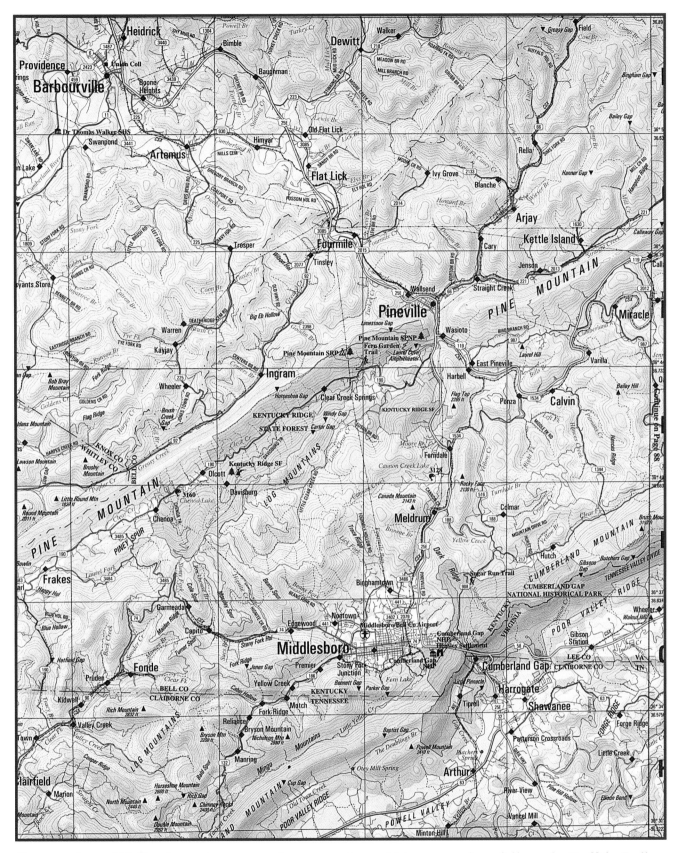

One can trace Walker's route on a modern map: he and his companions followed a Buffalo-Indian trail beginning about *Shawnee-Harrogate*. Descending from the saddle of Cumberland Gap, they followed *Yellow Creek* about twelve miles to *Clear Creek*, where they camped. Walker went hunting down the Creek and found that it joined a river which he named **"Cumberland"** *[near Wasioto]*. They went through Pine Mountain Gap to Cumberland Ford *[Pineville]*, but remained on the south bank of the river. They built a tiny cabin a few miles southeast of *Barbourville*.

"Doctor Walker, An English Chap"

The Cumberland Gap area is rich in folk traditions derived from immigrants from England and Ulster ("Scotch-Irish"). Speech patterns, songs, and folklore brought with them molded the culture of the pioneers who made new homes in the Southern Highlands.

This material was collected most notably by Cecil J. Sharp. Best-known is his *English Folksongs of the Southern Appalachians* [1932]. Loyal Jones of Berea College and others examine this material in a systematic way. Mountain culture also enriches novels by James Still, Harriet Arnow, Jesse Stuart and others.

High mountains, thick woods, narrow valleys, and gaunt ridges, made for isolation. Family and kin became vital for sheer survival. Roads were poor or non-existent, and for a century or more the mountain people were cut off from the mainstream of American life. But they made do, using every bit of their environment, for housing, for food, and for medicine. History, gossip, sermons, jokes, tales of ghosts and badmen, and stories of eccentricities and feuds, were preserved by settlers whose memories were the archive of tradition.

Music was part of everyday life. Mountain people hand-crafted banjos, fiddles and dulcimers, with rhythm provided by clapping, foot-stomping, jaw harp, jugs, spoons, wash-boards, and washtub bass. Songs, often religious tunes, enriched every occasion. Cumberland Mountain ballads, lyrical and social songs, worksongs, hollers and blues endured. Renamed "Bluegrass" by Bill Monroe in 1938, it is today an integral part of American culture.

Three anthologies -- *Sacred Harp, Kentucky Harmony, Harp of Columbia*, all scored in shaped notes -- are reprinted often, and "white spirituals" are a topic of academic study. Traditional melodies (sometimes revised or embellished with yodels and a "high-lonesome" wail) such as "Troubled in Mind," and "Has Anybody Seen My Lord," are known and sung throughout the mountains. Non-religious songs, such as "Dis Ol' Hammer," "Joe Turner," and "Make Me a Pallet on the Floor," were known by all.

Harvey H. Fuson, in *Ballads of the Kentucky Highlands* [1931], writes: "An old fiddler sits in the door of his cabin at the foot of the hill; he slowly draws the bow across the strings and looks away into the distance. He sings the songs that have come down to him from the remote past — `Sourwood Mountain,' `Barbara Allen' — because he enjoys them."

Cumberland Gap National Historical Park displays many physical artifacts of early pioneer culture. But one artifact can only be heard: it is a recorded performance of Billy Edd Wheeler singing "The Cumberland Gap."

The song was heard around the campfires of S.P. Carter's regiment, formed near Barbourville. Sam Lambdin, a left-handed fiddler from "The Gourd" section of the Clinch River, was a Union solider at the historic Gap. Soldiers, many Volunteers from the mountains of East Tennessee, were so pleased by the melody they bought the composer a new fiddle, and spread the song as they returned home. Lambdin was captured at the battle of Murfreesboro, his fiddle was seized, and he grew ill and died. Fuson writes: "There are different versions of this square dance; here is the one recognized by our old-time fiddlers."

The first white man in Cumberland Gap,
(repeat three times)
Was Doctor Walker, an English chap,
Lay down boys and take a little nap,
They're raising hell in Cumberland Gap.

■

"Daniel Boone Escorting Settlers through the Cumberland Gap," painted 1851-52 by George Caleb Bingham, is one of the most famous depictions of Boone and of The Gap. Bingham suggests that Boone was a kind of Moses -- no coonskin cap but a dignified beaver-felt hat -- leading settlers to "The Promised Land" of Kentucky. Bingham grew up on the Lewis and Clark trail in Missouri. He became an itinerant frontier preacher and an excellent portrait and landscape painter, mostly self-taught. He later entered politics.

Who Named Cumberland Gap?

Walker named many geographical features, though only a few "took" and most cannot be found in a modern gazetteer. Ambrose Powell, surveyor of Culpeper County and the most prominent member of Walker's 1750 party, may have given his name to Powell River, the one Walker called "Beargrass." One of his party gave his name to "Tomlinson's river," now simply the middle fork of the Kentucky, and Lawless gave his name to the north fork. Walker named the Louisa river [Tug Fork of The Big Sandy] after the sister of the Duke of Cumberland.

"Cumberland" is now of course a gap, a river, a mountain, a college, and a plateau. William Augustus, Duke of Cumberland and second son of George II and Queen Caroline, was known to Scots as "Willy the Butcher." But Walker was impressed by his victory at Culloden in 1746.

Lyman C. Draper, who amassed the definitive collection of 18th-century frontier memorabilia by acquiring (allegedly by theft, if necessary) every scrap of history that wasn't nailed down, verified the naming by Walker's affidavit to Judge Hall, and Walker's statement to Isaac Shelby. Walker told Shelby on Yellow Creek in 1770: "yonder beech tree contains the record of it. Ambrose marked his name and the year upon it, and you will find it there now. Shelby examined the tree and found large legible letters "A. Powell - 1750."

"Affidavits" did not persuade Theodore Roosevelt. His book, *Winning of the West*, says Walker found and named Cumberland Gap -- but NOT in 1750; he says Walker named it during the 1748 Woods River Land expedition of Colonel James Patton. The group included Walker and a retinue of servants, hunters, woodsmen, horses, and hunting dogs. They reached the middle fork of the Holston River.

During this trip Walker met Samuel Stalnaker, a trader with the Cherokee, who was an important informant for Walker in 1750. There is another contender: Patricia Givens Johnson, in *James Patton and the Appalachian Colonists,* reports the Patton family tradition that their ancestor discovered and named Cumberland Gap in 1748.

When Walker heard of Christopher Gist's explorations for The Ohio Company and of the fine plain of bluegrass, he undertook another trip — August 8 to September 18, 1751. The group passed through Cumberland Gap and found land suitable for settlement on both sides of "Dick's River," a north-flowing tributary of the Kentucky River that Walker named after a friendly Indian, Chief Dick. Walker made one other visit to the Dick's River area in either 1758 or 1760.

More exploration was planned. His fellow "Albemarle Adventurer," Colonel Joshua Fry, became convinced that passage to the Pacific was possible using the western tributaries of the Mississippi. The exploration was planned in detail and Walker was chosen as leader.

Preparation was well in hand when planning was halted by the outbreak of the French and Indian War. That Walker was chosen for such a vast project suggests the trust he enjoyed from his contemporaries and their confidence in his leadership and ability. ■

> **Journal, June 11, 1750:** *"We lost a Tomohawk and a Cann by the flood."*

AMAZING, IF TRUE

In 1845, a young man named Stopher found a fine tomahawk, a leather shot pouch, the remains of a powder horn and an Indian pipe under the west bank of the Salt River in Mercer County, Kentucky. The weapons had apparently been found by Indians in a swollen branch of the Big Sandy river, and were left behind following an Indian raid on Harrodsburg. Still sharp and in perfect condition, the tomahawk had the name "Thomas Walker" carved clearly on one side.

[Adapted from Nyland.]

"Pillar of Hercules" in Cudjo's Cave, Cumberland Gap National Historical Park. The Park plans guided lantern tours. King Solomon's and Soldier's Caves are connected; their total length is about seven miles, making it the 95th longest in the U.S. Both have 50-foot ceilings, fern-like crystals, straw-shaped stalactites, and colorful dripstone and flowstone.

The West Starts Here

> "Stand at Cumberland Gap and watch the procession of civilization, marching single file — the buffalo following the trail to the salt springs, the Indian, the fur-trader and hunter, the cattle-raiser, the pioneer farmer -- and the frontier has passed by."
>
> [Frederick Jackson Turner, 1893]

"The Way West" began at Cumberland Gap

By the end of the Revolutionary War, 200,000 settlers had crossed into the new territory. In the 1790s Wilderness Road traffic increased and the population continued to grow. Kentucky was admitted to the Union in 1792; by 1800 over 300,000 people had traversed the Gap, the Narrows and The Ford into Kentucky. In addition, thousands of cattle, sheep, pigs and turkeys were driven to markets in the east. As it had always been, the Gap was the key to commerce and transportation. In the 1820's and 1830's canals, and steamboats on the Ohio and Mississippi, began to offer an easier route, and the Gap declined in importance.

Cumberland Gap National Historical Park

The mission of America's largest national historical park is to stimulate the imagination and help visitors understand this interesting and important chapter of our country's history. But it's not easy to compete with superhighways.

The Park must somehow lure people out of cars and entice them to linger awhile and LOOK. That is the only way the significance of this place can be understood.

The Park extends along the crest of Cumberland Mountain including parts of Virginia, Kentucky and Tennessee. The three States join at the Gap. The Park comprises 20,305 acres, 80 per cent without paved roads. It is a place of significant history -- and of rugged wilderness beauty, with miles of trails, ranging from easy half-day

nature hikes to challenging overnight camping. The 21-mile Ridge Trail runs the length of the Park from the breathtaking Pinnacle vista, to Ewing, Virginia. The "White Rocks" at Ewing were a landmark for pioneers traveling the Wilderness Road.

Indian Rocks is a vast area littered with flint and stone where Indians once flaked their arrows and spears. Sand Cave, with an opening 240-feet wide and 80-feet tall, has a sand floor of 1.5 acres, and a seasonal 100-foot waterfall. A restored log cabin at Martins Fork, a Kentucky "Wild River," overlooks thick stands of rhododendron and towering hemlocks. Wildlife includes deer, black bear, bobcat, red fox, and 115 species of birds -- wild turkey, marsh hawk, ruffed grouse, and an occasional bald eagle.

The Park has 35 employees and an annual budget of $1.7 million. It attracts over a million and half visitors a year, and the number is growing. Now that the highway goes **under** the Gap, the Park has begun a major restoration project, thanks to funds secured by Congressman Harold Rogers. Graffiti will be removed from Cudjo's Cave ["Cave Gap"] so it will resemble its original "wild" state. More importantly, the Park will restore a portion of The Wilderness Road to the way it probably looked in 1780-1810, the era most representative of western expansion. The project will cost about $10 million, the largest restoration ever undertaken by the National Park Service. Work will be completed by 2003.

Boone and the pioneers would be proud.■

1. Original Grade

2. Bison/Indian Path

3. Indian/Explorer/Longhunter Path

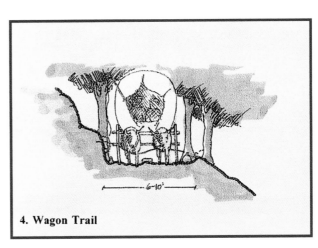

4. Wagon Trail

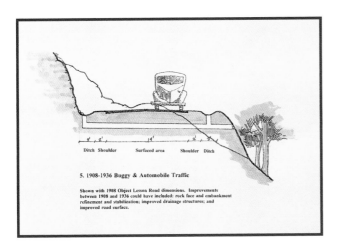

5. 1908-1936 Buggy & Automobile Traffic

Shown with 1908 Object Lesson Road dimensions. Improvements between 1908 and 1936 could have included: rock face and embankment refinement and stabilization; improved drainage structures; and improved road surface.

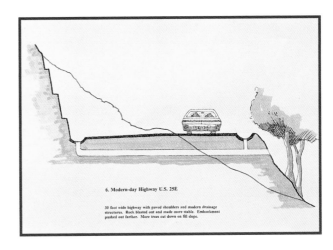

6. Modern-day Highway U.S. 25E

30 foot wide highway with paved shoulders and modern drainage structures. Rock blasted out and made more stable. Embankment pushed out farther. More trees cut down on fill slope.

The Wilderness Road evolved over many centuries. It was first a forest trail used by animals both extinct and modern, then a segment of "The Warrior's Path" used by a number of Indian tribes. The trail was later used by Long Hunters seeking game and valuable fur pelts. Beginning about 1775, it was used by pack-horses carrying pioneer settlers and their belongings. After 1800 there was an increasing number of wagons. By 1920 the ancient animal path had evolved into a modern paved highway, U.S. 25E.

Make It Yourself, Or Do Without

One of the most interesting features of Cumberland Gap National Historical Park is a group of farmsteads on a high plateau. Hensley Settlement shows what life was like for the pioneers who followed The Wilderness Road.

> **Life in rural Appalachia was hard and required work from dawn to dusk.**

Sherman Hensely founded The Settlement in 1903. He was the last person to leave the mountain in 1951 after living there two years by himself. The Settlement flourished for more than four decades. But during the late 1940's and early 1950's people began to leave, farms were abandoned, buildings deteriorated.

The area consists of five hundred acres at an elevation of more than three thousand feet. It can be reached by the Ridge Trail along Cumberland Mountain, or with a four-wheel drive vehicle via Brownie's Creek Primitive Road.

Because it was so isolated and remote — no roads, no electricity, access by foot or horseback only — the pattern of life was virtually identical to that of pioneer settlers a hundred or fifty years earlier.

The Park saw this as a rare chance to "go back in time." Visitors could understand the self-sufficient pioneers — a way of life kept alive at Hensley Settlement. Since 1965 the Park has restored three of the farmsteads with their houses, barns, fences, and fields, as well as the schoolhouse and cemetery. Two farmer-demonstrators maintain the buildings and fields, using techniques practiced by the Hensleys themselves.

Sherman Hensley and his family, and his in-laws the Gibbons family, were the mainstays of the Settlement. They cut down trees and cleared rocks and stumps for plowing. They hewed chestnut logs for cabins and farm buildings set on stone foundations, chinking gaps with mud. Roofs required two thousand split-cedar shakes; they split logs for fences; made most of their furniture; built fireplaces of stone, often serving for both heating and cooking. They needed many skills: how to tend animals, and grow, harvest, and preserve their food. The main crop was corn which for years they ground at their own mill, powered by water from a creek. They raised hay and fodder, and many kinds of vegetables. They grew grapes, and apples like limber twig and berry red -- dried or used for apple butter. Sheep wandered over mountain pastures: the wool was sold, or dyed and spun. Hundreds of hogs ran wild, subsisting on chestnut and hickory mast. They also kept cattle, oxen, horses, mules, and chickens. Late fall and winter was hog-killing time: meat was salted and preserved, fat rendered into lard, or used for soap.

The Hensely and Gibbons families made round hickory brooms, and bedding from corn shucks and goose feathers. They sewed quilts and most of their clothing. They used the special qualities of wood from trees like sourwood, black gum, linden, and basket oak. As the Indians before them, they used every thing the mountains offered — berries, honey, poke greens, and herbs like boneset, life everlasting, and seneca snakeroot.

They had to do many things our own generation has forgotten. They were carpenters who built their own cabins. They were black-smiths, shoeing horses and oxen. They made tools and were loggers and hunters. And they made whisky.

It's easy to romanticize rural Appalachia, and some have done so. In fact it was a hard life. Man, woman, child — young or old — worked from dawn to dusk. What they needed, they made or grew. They depended on each other, not the outside world.

For necessities they could not produce — "coal oil" for kerosene lanterns, shoes, iron kettles, some tools, material for clothing — they rode horseback or walked out and back over steep, narrow mountain trails. Heavy or bulky items were hauled up and down the mountain by mule- or ox-powered sleds. What little money there was came from selling wool, hogs, or game pelts. ∎

Log-cabin houses and farm buildings at Hensley Settlement, Cumberland Gap National Park. The Settlement is located on 500 acres on a plateau atop Cumberland Mountain [above 3,100 feet]. Because the area was so isolated -- no roads and extremely difficult access -- the families who lived there for forty years from 1903 until the late 40's had much in common with the self-sufficient subsistence farmers of Kentucky's pioneer days. A visit to Hensley Settlement is much like a trip back in time to about 1800.

Game, Land, Timber, Coal

Dr. Thomas Walker found eastern Kentucky covered with dense forests and filled with game. He also found coal. What he <u>sought</u> was fertile land. Settlers quickly shot out all the game, in some cases to extinction. Within weeks of arrival, settlers were often short of food and starving.

> **They shot out the game, cut down the timber, and ripped open the mountains for coal.**

Timber and coal followed the same pattern.

Loggers slashed through Kentucky's virgin timber with drunken abandon. Every year from 1870 to 1920 mountain raftsmen drifted millions of feet of prime logs downriver to be sold for pittances at sawmills. By 1930 most woodlands had been stripped: left behind were stumps and waste. The timber boom left nothing of lasting benefit — no furniture industry, no tradition of craftsmanship. Forest preservation and management began only <u>after</u> severe damage had been done. *[Adapted from Clark, pp 470-71]*

Regarding coal, The *Atlas of Kentucky* is succinct: "If the state has a resource cornucopia, it is in eastern Appalachia, an area that has experienced chronic poverty, yet produces a disproportionate share of the resource wealth, bituminous coal."

The story of coal in eastern Kentucky, or anywhere in Appalachia, is not clear or simple. It involves investments, jobs, labor conflicts and violence, boom-and-bust economics, and grief from accidents. Coal has affected the quality of life of thousands. The tentacles of the industry run deep into the lives of families, and into politics. Strip mining has removed mountaintops, choking creeks and valleys with debris.

The story is filled with emotions and contradictions, with no agreement even on basic facts. "To date there is no reliable history of the coal mining industry on which anybody, operators, miners, state officials, or general public, can base an intelligent understanding." *[Clark, p10]*

Rapid industrialization after the Civil War created an insatiable demand for coking coal to make steel. The vast coal fields of eastern Kentucky were known, but how to get the coal out? The answer: sharp lawyers who exploited the poverty and ignorance of the mountain people to acquire mineral rights, often at a dollar per acre, and a push for railroads to transport coal to the mills.

As railroads snaked along the valleys, isolated areas were transformed almost overnight. A valley with one lone cabin could become, in a few weeks, a booming coal town. The coal companies also brought schools, electricity, hospitals, motion-pictures, and stores. The coal-boom life held great appeal. Those who came in the first generation mostly did so eagerly. Mining seemed to offer a better life. One recalled: "I didn't have a choice. I had a family. They had to eat. You couldn't make a living on the farm." Would-be miners came from within the state, from across the region and from overseas. Immigrants and blacks added an ethnic mix to a population that had been almost totally Anglo-Saxon. In good years people had high wages, schools, medical care, and hope.

But wage jobs in the mines weakened the proud mountain tradition of self-sufficiency. Some coal companies controlled towns like little kingdoms. Miners were expected to vote as the company wanted; they paid high prices at company-owned stores; they were treated by doctors paid by the company; they lived where they were told; they were expected to be silent. They were largely controlled socially, physically, and psychologically by a corporation. *[Harrison, Klotter p308]*

Forests maimed by chestnut blight and get-it-all logging, are slowly recovering. Most of the coal camps are gone, but so too are the jobs. And in the wake of coal there is human damage — ex-miners, crippled, or dying of black lung disease. On the plus side, good roads and communication now connect a once-remote area to the world. But the most important resource in the region remains intangible: the intelligence and resilience of the people. That resource will determine the future. ■

COAL is Kentucky's most important mineral resource. Walker saw coal during his exploration, and brought back samples for fellow-investors in The Loyal Company.

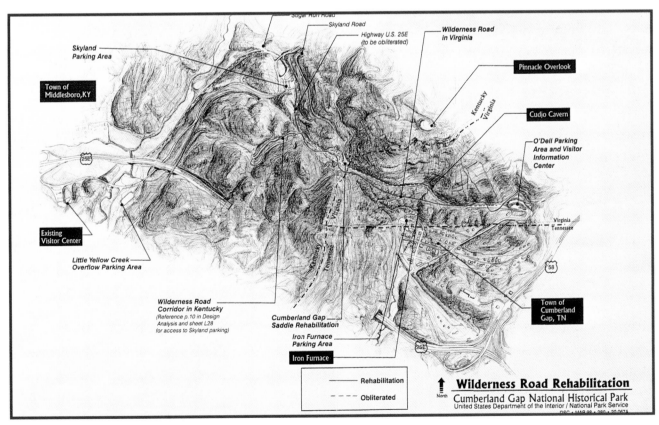

WILDERNESS ROAD rehabilitation will restore a portion of the Road to the way it would have looked in the period 1780-1810. Work will be completed in 2003.

Walker Would Be Amazed!

Walker and his group had tough going through the eastern Kentucky Wilderness. The Indian Road, often no more than a footpath, was choked by dense thickets of "laurel" (rhododendron), "ivy" (mountain laurel), and impassable bamboo-reed canebrakes. Walker wrote that they had to use "tomohawks" to clear a passage.

It seems fitting that a celebration started to honor Thomas Walker bears the name the Kentucky Mountain Laurel Festival. It is the oldest continuous event of its kind in the Commonwealth, started in 1931 by Annie Walker Burns, an enthusiastic (some might say indefatigable!) genealogist. While researching her own ancestors she became fascinated by Walker: she hoped she was descended from him, but was never able to make a clear connection. She did, however, compile several books, including an exhaustive family record published as *Doctor Thomas Walker, First White Man of Any Distinction to Explore Kentucky*.

Because of her energy and determination (and access to Governor Flem Sampson, for whom she worked), she was able to get things going. Dr. Thomas Walker had camped in 1750 at the site of Pineville. But few knew about him.

Shouldn't the State honor its first explorer? Shouldn't these beautiful mountains be the venue for the celebration?

The first two Festivals [1931 and 1932] were held at Clear Creek Baptist Bible College — an appropriate site, since Walker had camped on "Clover Creek" *[today, Clear Creek]*, which he followed it to its confluence with a river, which he named "Cumberland."

Mountain laurel is one of the great beauties of the Appalachian Spring, blooming in late May with spectacular clusters of pink or white flowers. This native shrub thrives in the moist, acidic soil of Eastern woodlands. The bark is scaly and reddish-brown. The leaves are poisonous, though deer seem immune. The Linnaean name is *Kalmia latifolia*; it is a member of the heath family. It was known to pioneers as "ivy" or "Spoonwood," ideal for making utensils.

In 1933 the event was moved to Laurel Cove Amphitheater in Pine Mountain State Resort Park. The Festival is held on the Memorial Day weekend. It attracts thousands of people — mainly from Kentucky, Virginia, and Tennessee, but also from across the country.

The Festival's center-piece is a pageant and the crowning of a Queen. All colleges and universities in Kentucky are invited to send candidates. There are usually fifteen or more — enough to be certain the honoree reflects the beauty of the mountains. The Queen is crowned by the Governor, who is rewarded by a buss on the cheek.

The Pageant follows the formalities of a royal coronation. It begins with a flag-raising, The National Anthem, the Lord's Prayer, and, of course, "My Old Kentucky Home." The court includes kindergarten-age pages; Junior High Princesses; and bearers carrying the Queen's train, crown, and ceremonial Pillow.

The Candidates then retire. There is a brief concert, while a secret committee chooses. The new Queen enters, preceded by gamely smiling, but unsuccessful, also-rans.

The Festival has a full agenda, with enough variety to appeal to every interest and age. A Gala Parade winds its way around Pineville's Courthouse Square: it features high school, university and military bands, coonskin-capped "pioneers," and colorful floats. There are also exhibits, contests and sports, including golfing, hiking, and marathon runs. There are arts and crafts displays and sales, church picnics and family reunions. And there is music and dancing of all kinds from gospel to swing to square and ballroom dancing. ■

The Kentucky Mountain Laurel Festival, held Memorial Day Weekend since 1931 (the oldest in Kentucky), celebrates The Beauty of the Mountains with a colorful parade, concerts, dances, folklore, golf and other sports, and family reunions. A Queen, chosen from colleges and universities through Kentucky, is crowned in lovely Laurel Cove amphitheater in Pine Mountain State Resort Park.

A Face-Lift for Clover Creek

After leaving Cave Gap, Walker and fellow-explorers followed the Indian Road down Flat Creek [today, *Yellow Creek*], camping there April 14, 1750. Millions of years ago Yellow Creek flowed south into the Powell river, carving a Gap in Cumberland Mountain. But the Mountain was uplifted faster than the creek's rate of erosion. At some point, the stream began to flow northward into the Cumberland.

Walker camped at what he calls "Clover Creek," a small stream at the base of Pine Mountain. Filson's map (1785) calls it "Buffalo Creek." Walker and Filson may have named the creek after *Buffalo Clover*, a plant now quite rare. The modern name is Clear Creek, the name in Daniel Smith's *Journal* of 1779 and Munsell's map of 1818.

Walker writes that the next day he went out hunting. He followed the Creek to its mouth, where it joined a river, which he named "The Cumberland." Over time, the name was given to the Gap, the Ford, the mountain, and the entire Southeastern Kentucky plateau.

Indians, Long Hunters, Walker, Boone, Henderson, and hundreds of thousands who followed The Warrior's Path and The Wilderness Road to Kentucky would still recognize Clover Creek and "the Narrows" Gap.

A ten-million dollar project to be completed in 2001 has dammed the stream to form a lake for limited fishing, water hazards for a 7,000-yard golf course, and water for greens. Bulldozers have gently smoothed every contour. The face-lift has created a golf course of great beauty. The mountain landscape endures.

Pine Mountain State Resort Park, Kentucky's oldest state park, opened in 1929 on land donated by the A.J. Asher family. One of the first features was a lake, created by damming the Creek, with 24 row-boats docked around a two-story pavilion. The centerpiece of the early Park was Laurel Cove, a natural amphitheater which since 1932 has been the site of the annual Kentucky Mountain Laurel Festival. The Cove is also used for concerts by the Lexington Philharmonic Orchestra, and was the setting (1959-1979) for a dramatic pageant, "*The Book of Job.*"

The park's first name was Cumberland State Park; it became Pine Mountain State Park in 1938, and decade by decade has been enlarged and upgraded. In the early 30's the Civilian Conservation Corps [CCC] built roads, foot-bridges, shelter houses, and scenic hiking trails of varying distances and difficulty. The Park comprises nearly 4,000 acres located within the 17,000-acre Kentucky Ridge Forest. Elevations range from 1,200 feet to 3,100 feet.

The CCC built the first lodgings — ten one-bedroom log cabins with stone fireplaces and private decks. Added later were ten two-bedroom cottages with screened porches, and modern conveniences. There are also 33 "primitive" campsites, a bathhouse, picnic shelter, playground, RV facilities, a nature center, gift shop, and naturalist programs. The lodge also displays the complete work of wildlife artist Ray Harm.

The CCC built the original Lodge of native sandstone rock and chestnut logs, arranged vertically. This remains the core, but The Lodge has been enlarged several times and now includes a dining room with a sweeping panorama of the southeastern slope of Pine Mountain, banquet and meeting rooms, a state-of-the-art convention center, a swimming pool, and thirty sleeping rooms.

Trails at Pine Mountain State Park wind through ravines of old-growth hemlocks, oaks and tulip poplar trees, fern gardens, waterfalls, lichen-covered boulders, and an ancient Indian "Rock Hotel." Catawba and Great rhododendron, red azalea, mountain laurel, pink lady's slipper and wild blueberry are scattered among serviceberry and flowering dogwood. The sandstone ridge at the top of the mountain includes Turtleback Rock and Chained Rock, with a dramatic view of Pine Mountain Gap, "The Great Pass." ∎

The Lodge at Pine Mountain State Resort Park [Pineville, Kentucky] has excellent meeting, lodging and dining facilities. The Park also offers exceptional panoramas of mountains, trees, flowers, birds and game. A beautiful new golf course opens in 2001.

Spectacular View To Honor Walker

Dr. Thomas Walker is remembered because he, unlike others who may have preceded him, kept a meticulous *Journal* of his exploration.

Judge William Ayers in a letter to *The Pineville Sun*, May 16, 1924 wrote: "Kentucky owes [Walker] much. But his story seems almost forgotten. It is my desire to honor his name and his five brave companions by the erection of a monument in the gorge at Pineville, the most appropriate location."

> **The Dr. Thomas Walker-Cumberland River Historic Site**
> was dedicated April 15, 2000

Annie Walker Burns proposed that Walker be honored by an annual event at Pineville. Her idea resulted in The Kentucky Mountain Laurel Festival, held continuously since 1931.

In 1994, the artist and writer, Richard Davis Golden, described in *The Pineville Sun* the importance of "The Narrows" and Cumberland Ford, both essential to The Wilderness Road and thousands of pioneer settlers. Golden proposed "a platform" to provide a view of the river's dramatic gorge. Golden's idea of an overlook was supported by the Bell County Historical Society. Jerry Browning, president of the Society, and others selected a "knob" with the most spectacular view. The 33-acre site, part of Pine Mountain State Resort Park, was expanded with the addition of land donated by Lowell and Roberta Turner. Browning, and Tom Shattuck and other Members of the Society, discussed the overlook proposal with John Brock, Park Superintendent. State officials in Frankfort gave permission for an Historic Site and "overlook," and Al Brock began construction of a parking lot and road. Larry and Virginia Giles laid out hiking trails up to the overlook site.

Today, the overlook offers a 360-degree view. To the North, one sees Clear Creek and the river. Walker's *Journal* entry, April 17, 1750: "Went down the Creek ... and found that it went into a River about a mile below our Camp. This ... I called Cumberland River."

Further North, one has a vista through "The Narrows," with Pineville *[Cumberland Ford]* and U.S. 25E going toward Flat Lick. What is alphalt today was first trod by wild animals and then Indians. The "Warrior's Path" became Boone's Trace, suitable for pack-horses. The path was continually improved, and by the mid-1790s, wagons could pass. In 1797 the Kentucky Legislature appropriated five hundred pounds for repair of The Wilderness Road at The Narrows and a toll-gate was built. This toll gate remained at The Gap until 1830 when it was moved to The Ford. The "Dixie Highway" passed through "The Narrows," as does today's superhighway.

Looking east, one sees Pine Mountain and Wasioto. [*"Ouasioto Mountains"* is the name on 18th-century maps of what geographers call The Cumberland Plateau.] Here in 1890, T.J. Asher built a sawmill and a railroad. Further east one sees majestic Little Black Mountain (2,948 feet).

Toward the southeast, one sees Cumberland Mountain and part of the National Historical Park. Looking southward, one sees Big Log Mountain and Little Clear Creek, and at the southwest point, Canada Mountain (2,143 feet).

Toward the West, one sees the mountain above Chenoa and the Henderson Settlement School. [*"Chenoa"* is an Indian name long associated with *"Ouasioto Mountains."*] The Site provides an unparalleled view of Pine Mountain and the scenic sandstone outcrop of "Chained Rock," a tourist attraction since 1931.

Parking for the Site is behind the Bert T. Combs building. Across U.S. 25E is a railroad spur (now a hiking trail) and the entrance to Pine Mountain State Resort Park, where a new addition to the Park, a splendid and beautiful new mountain golf course, will open in 2001. ∎

The Dr. Thomas Walker-Cumberland River Historic Site, above, is located off U.S. 25E. The Site honors the explorer and one of his most important discoveries. The Site is part of Pine Mountain State Resort Park. It offers a spectacular view of Pine Mountain Gap ["The Narrows" gorge], with panoramic vistas along Pine Mountain, the Cumberland River, and Clear Creek. The Site is on a "knob" at the northern end of Rocky Face Mountain, which follows the geologic fault which led to the creation of both Cumberland Gap and Pine Mountain Gap. The Site includes parking, lookout platforms, and a hiking trail. From this view, modern visitors, like Walker, Boone and thousands of pioneers who followed, can experience the drama of "The OTHER Cumberland Gap."

The Other Cumberland Gap

Kentucky's modern highways are a marvel. Today we can cruise from Lexington to Middlesboro at 60-plus. But speed may blind us to one of the most interesting and historically significant areas in America.

Daniel Boone and Cumberland Gap are known by all. But few have heard of Dr. Thomas Walker or of an equally-important but almost totally-ignored SECOND gap.

> **Cumberland Gap and Pine Mountain Gap formed TOGETHER a double natural GATEWAY to Kentucky's fertile Bluegrass.**

Dr. Thomas Walker, a Virginia physician, surveyor, and land speculator, was engaged by the Loyal Land Company to explore an 800,000-acre grant in the unknown "Wilderness" west of the mountains. Walker and five companions set out from Charlottesville in March 1750. They followed the valleys of the Shenandoah, Holston, Clinch, and Powell rivers.

Westward progress was blocked by a towering mountain of limestone, two thousand feet high, more than two hundred miles long. We know it as Cumberland Mountain. It was (and is) a daunting barrier. *To Walker, it seemed as impenetrable as The Great Wall of China.*

Walker and his party picked up trails trod by bison and elk, and by Indian hunters. These trails led up to a passageway through the mountains which Walker named Cave Gap. This "saddle" would later be called Cumberland Gap, and, along with the Ohio River, would provide one of two main routes into Kentucky.

The explorers were deterred after twelve miles by a SECOND Great Wall of rock just as high and long as the first. A creek ran along its base. On April 16, 1750, according to his *Journal*, Walker followed the creek to its confluence with a major river, which he named "The Cumberland."

The escarpments of the two mountains, straight as walls and almost as steep, were baffling barriers.

The Cumberland River had carved a deep gorge through Pine Mountain which allowed Walker and others to pass. Cumberland Gap and Pine Mountain Gap formed TOGETHER a double natural GATEWAY to Kentucky's fertile Bluegrass.

The "Water Gap" was a vital part of The Wilderness Road, and it remains a choke-point for all transportation. Indians called it *"Wasioto."* Pioneers called it "The Great Pass" and "The Narrows." Walker followed The Trail which led past a burial mound, and to a spot where the River could be forded easily.

John Finley, Daniel Boone's old comrade-in-arms from the French and Indian War, had entered Kentucky via the Ohio River. Back in North Carolina, he told Boone he had seen countless buffalo feeding on bamboo-like "cane," with herds of deer at every salt lick. The hunters could wait no more. And in 1769, Boone and Finley followed the Trail mapped nineteen years earlier by Dr. Thomas Walker. Cherokees from the South and Shawnees from the North gave **The Trail** its first name, "The Warriors Path." By 1770 it had become "The Longhunter's Trace." By 1780 it was "Boone Trace," then "The Wilderness Road," over which Boone and others led some 200,000 settlers into Kentucky. By 1920 "The Road" had become The Dixie Highway. Today it is U.S. 25E. "Cumberland Ford" is now Pineville, the site of the Mountain Laurel Festival and Pine Mountain State Resort Park. A Lodge overlooks beautiful forests and leafy trails. The Park will soon open a new world-class golf course. A nature preserve protects a sandstone shelter once inhabited by prehistoric people.

Stop and look at the spectacular canyon carved by The Cumberland through Pine Mountain. It's easy to see that the second gap -- "The OTHER Cumberland Gap" -- was vital to The Wilderness Road and to the settlement of the West. ■

"The Narrows" *[Pine Mountain Gap].* The Cumberland River has carved a deep and remarkable gorge through Pine Mountain -- the second, crucial "Gateway" which opened central Kentucky and the fertile Bluegrass to hundreds of thousands who traveled The Wilderness Road. Cumberland Ford was an equally important feature.

"Chained Rock" in Pine Mountain State Resort Park is a remarkable sandstone outcrop on the ridge of Pine Mountain. From here one has a magnificent view of The Narrows [Pine Mountain Gap], of Cumberland Ford *[Pineville, Kentucky],* and of an extraordinary natural passage through the mountain range. This Gateway was used by animals, Indians, hunters, pioneers, and today by railroads and superhighways. Visitors to The Narrows sometimes expressed apprehension that the rocks might fall. So, to create a little more tourist interest, a chain was hauled up the mountain by mule-teams and attached in 1931.

BIBLIOGRAPHY: Stephen E. Ambrose. *Undaunted Courage: Meriwether Lewis, Thomas Jefferson, and the Opening of the American West.* Simon & Schuster, NY, 1996; William Ayers. *Historical Sketches.* Pineville, KY, 1924-25; Bernard Bailyn. *The Peopling of British North America: An Introduction.* Vintage, NY, 1988, and *Voyagers to the East: A Passage in the Peopling of America on the Eve of The Revolution.* Vintage, NY, 1986; Bell County Hist. Soc. *History and Families: Bell County, KY.* Turner, Paducah, KY, 1994; Ted Franklin Belue, ed. *The Life of Daniel Boone by Lyman C. Draper, LL.D.*, Stackpole, Mechanicsburg, PA, 1998; Guy Meriwether Benson. *Exploring the West from Monticello: A Perspective in Maps from Columbus to Lewis and Clark.* U. of VA Library, 1995; Thomas D. Clark. *History of KY.* U. Press of KY, Lexington, 1937, 1992; *Frontier America: The Story of the Westward Movement;* and *Historic Maps of KY.* U. Press of KY, Lexington, 1979; William E. Cox. *Hensley Settlement: A Mountain Community.* Eastern Natl. Park & Monument Assoc. 1993; William Cronon. *Changes in the Land: Indians, Colonists, and the Ecology of New England.* Hill & Wang, NY, 1983; William P. Cummings. *The Southeast in Early Maps,* William M. Cummings, U. of NC Press, Chapel Hill 1986; Jared Diamond. *Guns, Germs, and Steel: The Fates of Human Societies.* Norton, New York, 1997. Natalie J. Disbrow. *Thomas Walker, Man of Affairs.* MA Thesis. U. of VA. 1940; John Mack Faragher. *Daniel Boone: The Life and Legend of an American Pioneer.* Henry Holt, NY, 1992; Craig Thompson Friend, ed. *The Buzzel About Kentuck: Settling the Promised Land.* U. Press of KY, Lexington, 1999; Daniel M. Friedenberg. *Life, Liberty and the Pursuit of Land: The Plunder of Early America.* Prometheus, Buffalo, NY, 1992; John Filson, *The Discovery, Settlement, and Present State of Kentucke.* James A. Frutchey. *Doctor Thomas Walker, Colonial Virginia's Extraordinary Entrepreneur.* MA Thesis. Pa. State U. 1968; Neal O. Hammon. "Early Roads Into KY," *Register* of the KY Hist. Soc. April 1970, pp. 91-131; Archibald Henderson. "Dr. Thomas Walker and the Loyal Company of Virginia," *Proceedings* of the American Antiquarian Society, Vol. 41, New Series, Part 1, April 15, 1931; H.H. Fuson. *Ballads of the KY Highlands.* Mitre Press, London, 1931; and "The Cumberland Ford Settlement: Paper Read Before The Filson Club." *KY Progress Magazine,* December 1930 and January 1931; *History of Bell County,* 1947. Lowell H. Harrison and James C. Klotter. *A New History of KY.* U. Press of KY, Lexington, 1997; Patricia Givens Johnson. *James Patton and the Appalachian Colonists.* Verona, VA, McClure Press, 1963; J. Stoddard Johnston. *First Explorations of KY.* (First Publ. Series, No. 13; Louisville: The Filson Club, 1889); Robert L. Kincaid. *The Wilderness Road.* LMU Press, Harrogate, TE 1955; John E. Kleber, ed. *The KY Encyclopedia.* U. Press of KY, Lexington, 1992; R. Barry Lewis. *KY Archaeology.* U. Press of KY, Lexington, 1996; *Magazine of Albemarle County History, Volume 52, 1994.* Albemarle County Hist. Soc. Charlottesville, VA, 1994; Alexander Canaday McLeod. "A Man For All Regions: Dr. Thomas Walker of Castle Hill." *The Filson Club History Quarterly,* Vol. 71, No. 2, April 1997, pp. 169-201; "Three Travelers on the Mississippi: George Rogers Clark, Thomas Walker, and Daniel Smith," *The Filson Club History Quarterly,* Vol. 73, No. 4, Oct. 1999, pp. 377-389; Colin McEvedy. John Hammond Moore. *Albemarle: Jefferson's County, 1927-1976.* Albemarle County Hist. Soc. 1976; W.E. Myer. *Trail System of the Southeastern United States in the Early Colonial Period.* Bureau of American Ethnology. 1923; Keith Ryan Nyland. *Doctor Thomas Walker (1715-1794): Explorer, Physician, Statesman, Surveyor and Planter of Virginia and KY.* PhD dissertation. Ohio State U. 1971; Charles Royster. *The Fabulous History of the Dismal Swamp Company: A Story of George Washington's Times.* Knopf, NY, 1999; Park Rouse, Jr. *The Great Wagon Road From Philadelphia to The South.* Dietz, NY, 1995; Martin F. Schmidt. *KY Illustrated: The First Hundred Years.* U. Press of KY, Lexington, 1992; Tom N. Shattuck. *A Cumberland Gap Area Guidebook.* Wilderness Road Tours, Middlesboro, KY, 1994; Paul D. Sifton, "The Walker-Washington Map," *Quarterly Journal of the Library of Congress,* April 1967; Thomas Speed. "The Wilderness Road ..." *The Filson Club;* William O. Steele. *The Old Wilderness Road: An American Journey.* Harcourt, Brace, NY, 1968; Frederick Jackson Turner. *Significance of the Frontier in American History;* Richard Ulack, ed. *Atlas of KY.* U. Press. of KY, 1998.

CREDITS: Cover: H. Tom Hall, *Into The Wilderness,* Natl. Geog. Books, 1978. p5 Proclamation, photo of Gov. Patton: Bob McDonald. p8 Don Chesnut, KY Geolog. Survey. p9 topo map, *Atlas of KY:* U. Press of KY. p12 Carey Tichenor, Chief Naturalist, KY Dept. of Parks. p14 whistle from burial mound, Pineville, KY: Fred Woods. p38 Washington's compass and drafting tools, Mount Vernon Ladies' Assoc. p39 Colonial Williamsburg Foundation. p49 Indian trail, Wilderness Road: Jack Collier, Cumberland Gap Natl Hist. Park and Tom Shattuck, Chairman, Bell County Tourism Comm. and Wilderness Road Tours, Middlesboro, KY (606) 248-2626. p 59 Castle Hill: VA Hist. Preservation Assoc. p65 courtesy Neal O. Hammon. pp70-71 Dennis Latta, George Rogers Clark NHP. p74 *Kentucky Explorer,* Oct. 1995, p63. p77 *KY Atlas* © DeLorme, Yarmouth, ME. p78 Richard K. Burns, Legacy Books, Hatboro, PA. p79 George Caleb Bingham, "Daniel Boone Escorting Settlers through the Cumberland Gap, 1851-52" Oil on canvas, 36.5 x 50.25" Washington U Gallery of Art, St. Louis, Gift of Nathaniel Phillips, 1890. p89 KY Mountain Laurel Festival, Pineville, KY (606) 337-6103. p99 map courtesy estate of Park Rouse Jr. All other photos by Adam Jones, except pp11, 47, 87 by David Burns.

DAVID BURNS spent his boyhood in Pineville, KY, and now lives in Washington, DC. His work has been published in *The Washington Post, Los Angeles Times, New York Times, Wall Street Journal* and many other newspapers and magazines. He was Director (1978-90) of the Climate Proj., Amer. Assoc. for the Advancement of Science, editing 12 scientific studies. He was a Foreign Service Officer (1955-78) at U.S. embassies in Damascus, Beirut, Isfahan, Rhodesia, Tunis, Bamako, Algiers; he studied Arabic in Tangier, Morocco. He graduated from Princeton, studied in France on a Fulbright grant and at Johns Hopkins and Howard Universities. He worked (1943-46) in the U.S. Senate under the patronage of Sen. Alben Barkley, and moonlighted as a copyboy (1944-46) for *The Washington Star.* He served in the U.S. Air Force 1946-49. He leads a jazz quintet which has recorded four LPs and three CDs. "**THANKS** to Jerry Browning, fellow-Members of the Bell County Historical Society, all librarians esp. Ron Day; thanks to Alex McLeod, Frank Doughman, Jack Collier, John Taylor and others who patiently responded to my queries. Stoff Smulson did the portrait above. I'm deeply grateful for the extra-ordinary support of my wife, Sandy and my son, Patrick. And the magisterial artistry of Adam Jones who makes words superfluous."

ADAM JONES has been a professional photographer for ten years. He lives in Louisville with his wife, Sherrie. He publishes travel, natural history, and how-to-articles in *Outdoor Photographer, Birder's World, Wildbird, Natural History, Petersen's Photographic, Audubon,* and other magazines. He won the In Praise of Plants category, BBC Wildlife Photographer 1994. He is an advisor for Natural Selection Stock of Photography, Rochester, NY. He leads tours and teaches workshops. Tel: (502) 327-0416. "**THANKS** to David Burns for having the confidence in me to complete this project on a tight deadline. I've developed a deep appreciation of the Pinevillle/Cumberland Gap area and am grateful for the generous support of John Brock, Al Brock, Dean Henson, Tom Shattuck, Sam & Missy Mayes, Dale & Wilma Benedict; Jerry Browning coordinated details and directed me to important areas. **TECHNICAL:** Cameras: Pentax 67 using 220 film and Pentax SMC 45mm, 55mm, 135mm and 200mm lenses. Many images were made in 35mm format [Canon EOS-3], lenses from 17mm to 800mm. Exposures were calculated in-camera on Fujichrome Professional 100 and Velvia film. Polarizing, slight warming, or neutral density filters were sometimes used. Support: Gitzo 320 tripod with a Bogen 3-way pan tilt head."

Cartouche from John Filson
Map of Kentucke (1784)

INDEX